WHAT KIND OF CHRISTIAN ARE YOU?

by Rickey Teems II (but mostly by God)

Dedicated to Amanah Rani Teems.

Watching you become a young adult has made me a better

Christian!

NoGuile Books
P.O. Box 30675
Los Angeles, CA 90030

www.noguilebooks.com

Cover Design by Maurice Scriber at http://mwsdesignz.com

Printed in the United States of America

Don't forget to visit www.noguilebooks.com for other great
reads!

Table of Contents

INTRODUCTION

What kind of Christian are you? Seems almost intrusive doesn't it? What would give *anyone* the right to ask such a direct question about your personal beliefs? Especially when it comes to religion! We all know some people can be so judgmental when it comes to talking about God, you would think they live in a courtroom! Plus, it's not like you are obligated to explain your spirituality to *anyone*, so why should *anyone* be allowed to ask what type of Christian you are! See, and you were worried about judging a book by its cover. But, actually, as I prayed and was motivated to write this book, I didn't have just *any one* in mind who might ask what type of Christian you are. I was thinking more about, The One! No, no, not Neo from the Matrix (even though he did free us all from the villainous machines). No, I was thinking of someone who saved us from something slightly more significant, and definitely more real, like the *only* one. Introducing (drum roll please, cue the palm branches, saddle up the donkey), Jeeeeeesuuuus! Seriously, think about it for a second. We all know how the typical religious debates go with other people, but what would your response be if Christ, himself, were to ask you about your faith and life in Him?

I know. A) We all have free will so it's not that we are obligated to even have a life in Him.
B) Since He *supposedly* knows everyone's heart, why would He need to ask? That would be worse than a "psychic" looking in the newspaper for lottery number predictions. But the more I thought about it, the more I realized that maybe Jesus is asking each of us about our faith in Him– like every day, whether we believe in Him or not.

From the moment we wake up, well, maybe not right when we wake up. Some of us need to hit the snooze button a few times, others need Starbucks or energy drink first.

Okay, but at some point, once we actually get up, our minds shift into gear and begin to evaluate the day and possible decisions and actions we may have to take. Do you think of the positive opportunities first? Are you a believer who thanks God first and foremost for the blessing of another day and His infinite possibilities? Or do you drag out of bed, miserable, complaining before you even get rid of your morning breath? Dreading school or work? When situations and circumstances arise, hearing gossip about yourself, temptations, someone cutting you off in traffic, someone on the corner asking for spare change, how do you respond? There are no right or wrong answers, and these examples barely scratch the surface of what most of us deal with personally throughout the day, but no matter what, your reactions always clarify one thing, what kind of Christian you are, if one at all. Could God be placing you in different scenarios to prove what kind of Christian you are through actions, rather than words or cool T-shirts? You better believe it! So really, Christ is asking what kind of Christians we are by seeing how closely our thoughts and actions follow His teachings and the examples He left when it comes to our own everyday lives (not just church on Sundays).

What kind of Christian are you? There is always the possibility someone is asking you this question in reference to denomination. You know, Baptist, Presbyterian, Episcopal, Lutheran, or any of the other five million distinct beliefs based on different interpretations of biblical scriptures. Okay, 5 mil may be a teeny exaggeration, but it doesn't matter anyway, because we won't be discussing any specific denominations in this book. It's not that they aren't important to understand or that I have a problem with any of them, it's just that at least 8 out of 10 people who ask what kind of Christian you are, probably aren't referring to denomination.

No, if you're fortunate for someone to ask you what kind of Christian you are to your face (as more often than not it will probably be asked behind your back with a lot of skepticism) it is because they are probably referring to some behavior or characteristic they don't think is, "Christian-like."

Hypocrite! No, I'm not calling you one, but this is undoubtedly the most used adjective when it comes to people who don't completely understand Christianity and always question why Christians don't perfectly embody every biblical principle, and why we make mistakes, and why we aren't always nice 'n giving, and why we sometimes have bad days, and why we have made decisions we regret but can't change the past, and why we sometimes want to scream, "JUST LEAVE ME ALONE!" And you know, all those other things that make us, well, to be honest– human. But notice I said, "people who don't completely understand Christianity?" It's not just non-Christians who throw judgment around, some Christians and churchgoers are pretty good **gavel bangers** too. Which is ironic, because by judging others that actually makes them just as much of a hypocrite, but we'll talk about that later. What all of those people, Christian or not, fail to realize, is that if any of us were able to do 100% of everything God commands in the bible, we wouldn't need Christ's grace anymore. It would be called, (your name here) anity! Not being perfect doesn't make anyone a hypocrite, it helps us realize we would have been much better off discovering Christ a whole lot sooner! We recognize the need for change and salvation, but understand it's not an overnight process.

Oh, by the way, **gavel bangers = "Those who tend to hold an unrealistic view of how Christians should act, and are more focused on judging others, even though the court was closed centuries ago when Jesus died for us."** *From time to time you may see some very articulate and genius terminology (that I literally just made up) like, gavel banger. If you aren't sure what it means, check the back of the book in the reference pages for a quick definition.*

So let's face it, usually when people ask, "What kind of a Christian are you?" it has a very negative tone. After all, if they didn't think we were doing anything wrong as Christians, they wouldn't need to inquire. You don't ask a fireman who just rescued a family from a burning building and singlehandedly put out the fire, "What kind of fireman are you?" You wouldn't need to. His exemplary actions proved that he is committed. But you may ask that question of the fireman who never responds to any calls and just lazily sits in the station collecting a paycheck. It's kind of similar with Christianity. People usually only question what kind of Christian you are after you have made some sort of mistake or they think there is something you are doing wrong. And it's not whether you actually are or aren't, it's just their own misdiagnosis. But the purpose of this book isn't to help you deal with negative people, otherwise it would never end! It's also not to help you judge them in return once you have a more confident understanding. And it is definitely not to question whether you are a real Christian or not. That's between you and God.

The true purpose of this book is to help both non-believers and believers understand that Christianity is not just a one time triumph or title that we wave as a badge. Christianity should be a progression of spiritual growth and maturity where you achieve new levels of faith and blessings over time, a lifetime to be exact.

Still, some may say argue there are no levels to Christianity and there is only one kind of Christian– saved. Meaning, if you have claimed Jesus to be your Lord and Savior, then you are a Christian, and nothing else matters. That's partly true. But remember, *Christian* actually means, *like Christ*.

So if being a Christian means being like Christ, the first thing we have to do is? Any guesses? Anyone? How about you? Yes you, reading the book. That's right!! We must first learn what Christ was like, then we must learn how to apply it to our own unique personalities and purposes. It's safe to say that despite our strengths, there are a number of areas all of us have that will need improvement. That is where this book comes into play. What kind of Christian are you, will look at seven general categories of believers. Remember, these aren't denominations, tribes from the bible, or anything technical. They are just the most common groups many of us have encountered in our own spiritual walks. And yes, there may be some qualities or issues that span across multiple groups. There may be some people that are hard to classify as any one particular type because they fit a little bit of several. That's fine. This book wasn't written to judge or label anyone specific. So please don't go running out and calling people names from this book and telling them I said it was okay. I don't want to have to run from an angry mob in the mall parking lot if I happen to be in your city.

In the interest of complex simplicity, this book is merely a guide to help us recognize that we are all at different points in our spiritual journey, and God is okay with that. BUT, if we want to go farther in our understanding and Christian walk, then knowing where we are currently and which direction we need to be headed is critical to reaching our true purpose.

Another quick FYI, disclaimer, notice, whatever, this book isn't designed to cover every looming question surrounding the religious beliefs of Christianity. There are people far more qualified, ordained, experienced, enlightened, and good ol' fashioned smarter, who can make that graceful swan dive from the high dive if we're looking to go in the deep end.

Honestly, this book is probably more of a cannon ball in the kiddie pool! Sorry to disappoint any of you, "oh ye great philosophical and religious debaters," but your books were probably one shelf up. This is a friendly discussion on some of the basics, to hopefully encourage increased reading and learning about Christianity for everyone on every level. So please read through all of the categories, even if you absolutely do not fit it, because who knows what you may learn and how you might be able to help someone else with the knowledge. One thing is for certain, God loves us all and can work through us no matter what level we're on!

NOT
I don't follow Christ

Well, the good thing is, it is still very very early in the book, so you haven't wasted too much time on something you will not like and will never believe. Although, what if there was like a .00001% chance this wasn't a waste of time? You obviously opened the book up for a reason, and just because you don't believe in Christ doesn't mean you don't believe in knowledge, intelligence, insight, learning, growth, maturity, creation, love, life, morals, and pretty much everything many Christians claim can only happen through Christ.

I'll be the first to admit, we Christians can be the most judgmental people that are clearly instructed not to be judgmental...and yet are still ridiculously judgmental! #NoGavels

Many are quick to assume that just because you don't believe in Jesus Christ means you are incapable of knowing anything whatsoever. As if your brain doesn't work unless it's jumpstarted with a little holy water from a baptism!

I don't blame you for being disgusted. If people routinely belittled my intelligence because of their own personal beliefs, or were so one-track minded it wasn't even worth having a discussion with them, I'd pretty much write them off too. And that's just attitude and dialogue! How about that bible we believe in?! The history of carnage against mankind in the name of *God*! A God so loving He flooded and killed the entire planet! He rained down fire and destroyed an entire city! He told Abraham to kill his own son! Not to mention, how are you supposed to believe in the bible and a God nobody can see, when evolutionism has been scientifically proven? Some of you may even believe in God, but don't believe that Christ is the only way to get to Him. So you're asking, what makes Christianity so special? Every religion says it is the best.

All of these are relevant questions. Let's face it, if Christians are going to ask you to believe in something, the very least we could do is allow you to ask questions and understand what we want you to believe, right? But nooo. **We wanna preach how much God loves you, how bad we want to pray for you and point out biblical scriptures (as if doctrine from something you already don't follow makes it more convincing). But the second you ask one little question, all that Godly love turns into the devil's wrath as we argue and fight with you how our way is the only way, and you'll spend eternity in hell if you do not follow our rules immediately.** Honestly, I have to agree with you.

<u>If those are the type people that are gonna be at the party, I'm not RSVPing either!</u> #NoThanks!

If it makes you feel better, I could give you a big melodramatic apology on behalf of all the real Christians that have ever lived. I could go on and on how wrong other Christians were and how that should never have happened because that's not what Christ teaches us, but I'm pretty sure that's not what you want. Not to mention, we will address those types of Christian behaviors in later chapters, but I still have absolutely no way of controlling if some people will continue to act like the above. Although, between you and me, it is my secret hope that every person on the planet will read this book and every offensive religious debate and war will forever cease. Maybe I'll win something really cool like a Nobel Peace Prize or free Chick-a-Filet!

Like I said, I don't think you want an apology. I think you want an honest conversation where you aren't judged for believing differently. I think you want to see people exemplify what it is they profess to follow!

I think you want to be left alone and not hounded as if you are the worst person ever born for not believing in something just for the sake of doing it. #Choice

Now, if you still want to have that conversation, please read on. But let's be clear, I'm not making excuses or asking you to accept anything. Everyone reading this will be at different points in life, some may not believe in Christ, but believe in a higher power or being. Some may be Agnostic or Atheist. Some may be members of a different religion, so please remember this wasn't written for the most intense religious debates. Merely providing a perspective, hopefully alternative, for you to consider about Christianity.

I'll admit, I don't know everything there is know about God or the bible. But isn't that one of the biggest flaws of Christianity? *People not being able to admit they don't have all the answers, then getting upset when your questions back them into a corner.* Well, I guess that's as good of a place to start as any. The first thing to realize, as I'm sure you have figured out by now, is that **Christians are not perfect.** Passionate? Obviously. Perfect? Far from it! So why do they act that way? Why do they come across more like trial attorneys than saints? I think it all starts with understanding attachment. Think back to the first thing you felt you absolutely could not live without. Maybe it was a toy, a blanket, your parents/guardian, a boyfriend/girlfriend, a car, whatever it was, we have all had some person or thing that consumed our thoughts nearly every second of the day. We didn't want to sleep. When we did sleep, we couldn't wait to wake up. Couldn't focus on anything else and we wanted the rest of the world to know it! Now take that same feeling and magnify it by like, infinity! That's what Christians feel about Christ.

Though we don't always act like it, from a Christian standpoint we feel we have discovered the real secret to peace and happiness, achieving our greatest potential, and making it to heaven when this life is no more. And we found all of this without having to pay $19.95 plus shipping and handling for some infomercial product that will only work for a couple of weeks. We're excited! We're revitalized! We want to share how our lives have changed and allow everyone to feel the same completeness. Unfortunately what many of us don't realize is that our happiness may not be the same fountain of fun for everybody. We want others to share our joy, but only on our terms. **Good intentions, horrible approach.**

The other primary issue you have probably had when dealing with Christians is the biblical direction for us to – spread the word of God in hopes that others will believe and become saved through Christ – a civic duty if you will. Which is fine, except many of us seem to forget that another part of the bible clearly states that God has given everybody free will to choose or reject a Christian lifestyle. So rather than getting offended or forceful when sharing the bible, Christians should just walk away if a person isn't interested. If you aren't familiar with the bible, God never instructed us to argue and fight with people on his behalf. He isn't a boxing promoter! In fact God says the exact opposite of how many Christians actually act. We are told that not everybody will believe. We are told to act in love and patience. We are told to shake the dust off our feet when people don't want to hear what we have to say. So why do Christians continue to force their salvation on others? I think the answer to that question will be as numerous as the Christians who do it, but here are some general possibilities:

1) Believe they are doing the right thing.

2) Genuinely concerned about you and what happens after death.

3) Pride, think they are a better Christian if they stand up for God.

4) Pride (yep, again), think they are better than everybody else because they are Christian.

5) Status, think they will be a better Christian if they convert more people.

6) Ignorant, you'd be surprised how many Christians don't act "Christ like" because they haven't even read the bible to know how Christ acted, or understand keeping their evangelism in check.

7) Obsession, I'm not saying this to be cruel or humorous, but just because a person is a Christian doesn't mean they are completely mentally stable. Christians aren't immune to the occasional crazy. But please save the psych evals for trained and educated professionals.

These are only a few possibilities of why Christians may go against the biblical grain, but no matter the reason or sincerity, they are wrong for trying to force their beliefs on you or anyone. But negative Christian attitudes aren't the sole reason why some people don't believe in Christ. In many instances, Christians have nothing whatsoever to do with it. It's the doctrine itself that turns some off. How can we know the bible is real? If God is so loving, why did he destroy the planet with Noah's ARC? How come Christianity doesn't accept other religions? How come Christians don't accept evolution? These are just a few of the questions many people have when it comes to the beliefs and doctrines of Christianity.

<u>It doesn't seem like one little book, that was obviously meant to help those who believe in it, could cause so much worldly and historic confusion, division, and even harm.</u> #UnintendedConsequences

Many blame the bible for wars, death, and atrocities dating back to the earliest of civilizations to now. *What do you mean, blame the bible? Are you saying it's not responsible?* That may be what you are asking, but that's not what I'm saying. To be fair, for this particular chapter, **I think we have to separate the questions that apply to the text of the bible and those that apply to interpretation of the text of the bible.** For example, many say the bible contradicts itself. One part says God loves everyone unconditionally, but another says he wiped out the planet with a flood. That is a fair bible assessment based on the text. It is written in black and white for all to see in the book of Genesis. However, "how come Christians hate other religions?" isn't a fair biblical question, because a) it is not written anywhere in the bible and b) not all Christians do. Since that is a matter of interpretation and personal preference, it would require every single person to give their own account of why – which would take time neither you nor I have (and probably wouldn't want to give if we did). Not to mention, it would basically render the subtitle, *"short and sweet,"* inaccurate. And nobody likes an inaccurate subtitle. It can really mess up your day.

Despite the millions of questions and debates regarding the bible, without a doubt, the one central mystery has to be, how do we know the bible is real? We could talk about all the things that happen in the bible, the rules and commandments, the unexplainable miracles, the spiritual entities, but what does any of that matter if you don't first believe that the bible is real? That's the equivalent of debating what a unicorn's horn is made of, only to later admit you don't believe unicorns exist anyway. Make sense? So how do we know the bible is real? Well, just go to any bookstore or hotel nightstand, you'll see it, Holy Bible.

Oh, we weren't talking about *real* as in physical existence? We meant real as in content. Gotcha. LOL. Seriously, you aren't alone for asking this question. To be honest, there are Christians who have their doubts too, which we will cover in later chapters. But from your standpoint, it's usually less about faith, which is a Christian thing, and more about empirical or scientific proof, right? I guess the starting point for this answer is understanding the bible isn't just one book. **Many people assume the bible is just one big story written by Christians to glorify Christianity.** The reality is that the bible is really several books that span over centuries from different regions that were all carefully selected and pieced together, and, no, they weren't all written by Christians. In fact, most of it wasn't written by Christians at all, and none of it was written by Jesus.

Far before Christianity and the bible as we know it today, various forms of religion have always existed in most societies. Whether it was polytheistic (meaning multiple Gods), monotheistic (meaning one God), the worship of deceased family members, the worship of idols, animals, supernatural powers, you name it, it has probably been worshipped. From fertility to food to fear, there have been uncountable reasons why people have believed in higher powers. There is no consensus to the exact roots of religion, but we do know that 'organized' religion, what we know today, became more popular as writing emerged as a more primary form of communication and larger empires began to dominate their lands. *Rickey, great, but why are you boring me with this history lesson?*

Christianity is one of the most recognized forms of organized religion, especially here in America and other Western civilizations. Some tend to base their knowledge of Christianity strictly on the bible. But it's important to realize that the bible itself wasn't the first writing on Christianity. As I stated earlier, the bible is actually a collection of many books and letters. And it wasn't neighbors or people from the same church. We're talking writings from completely different eras and territories. What's even more relevant (and amazing) are the predictions that are made and actually come true, sometimes hundreds of years later. The ancient scrolls, found over time, organized into the Old and New Testaments that make up the bible today, were first interpreted into Greek, then later Latin, and eventually nearly every language known to mankind. And that's what happened with the formation of the bible. But what's more important, some events that the bible describes are also written about and confirmed in other documents of that time, by people that weren't even affiliated with the people of the bible.

We mentioned the bible being broken down into the Old and New testaments. Though the Old Testament transitions and sets the tone for Christianity, it is actually based on Judaism. Technically, Christianity didn't start until about half way through the New Testament. How is any of this relevant? What does it prove? Because of its complex origins, historical references, testing, mentions from outside sources and overall existence throughout various societies, very few historians doubt the bible is real. Even many non-Christian historical sources verify the legitimacy of the bible. **What is called into question, more often than not, are the supernatural or miraculous works written in the bible.** Did they really happen or are they just exaggerations? And if they did really happen, was it a Supreme Being (God), or are there some scientific explanations? Because the objective of this chapter isn't to convince you of miracles, those questions will be tackled in later chapters (Note to self, don't say later chapters any more).

When you think about it, even research it for yourself, the fact that the words that compose the bible have weathered religious history is somewhat impressive. There have been as many different belief systems as there have been societies, if not more. Judaism wasn't even a dominant religion to begin with, and during the time of Jesus, the Jews were under the powerful Roman rule, who had a completely different religious system. In fact, several times throughout their history the Jewish people were subjected by others, including Egypt, when it was common for the ruling party to force their religion onto those they conquered. So it is significant that the scrolls that later composed the bible not only endured those periods, (when many were trying to destroy or erase them from history) but have now risen to one of the most embraced religions worldwide. *Oh, that's only because it has been forced onto people like the Spanish Inquisitions and Roman Catholics did.* I have heard more than one person say this, but consider, if

Rome was one of the most dominant empires ever, how did Christianity even get through to them? They had their own beliefs already, not to mention, one of the largest, deadliest armies since the beginning of civilization! Romans controlled the lands where Christianity started with such an imposing military presence, the Jews lived in fear of them. So how did the Romans come to believe in Christianity so much they felt it should be the mandatory religion of the land they ruled? It's not like anyone could have forced or manipulated them to believe? That would have been impossible! Something had to have made them believe to that serious of an extent. And this isn't condoning the use of threats or pressuring people into religion, that is not what the bible instructs. I'm simply exploring why Christianity has penetrated so many minds and endured, when the odds were stacked against it, and so many other religions (that had military push or larger followings) have fallen off or not achieved any global significance. Food for thought.

Before they crucified Him, the powers-that-be planned very carefully to not have any magnification of Jesus' miracles and teachings after He was gone. They just wanted to spread a word that He was a crazy man with crazy followers and let the hype die out (ironic that 2014 years later the exact opposite happened and Christianity is one of the highest followed religions). So initially followers of Christ had to remember and honor Him in private because authorities would torture and kill anyone claiming to be one of His disciples. The recorded history of Christians suffering for their beliefs is not limited to the bible, non-religious accounts also corroborate that early Christians were brutalized in the worst way. The Romans had Christians massacred for sport in the famous

Roman Coliseum. They would have unarmed Christians fight bears and lions in front of huge crowds just for the blood bath.

Today, there are still parts of the world where Christians are arrested and even killed for their beliefs. The Freedom of Religion granted to many of us isn't practiced everywhere. In fact, some people's Christian commitments require them to risk their lives because of mandated religious systems still instituted by governments. It's true. In some areas just obtaining a bible can be unsafe. So what makes Christians risk their lives and families in these strict territories? Certainly Christianity isn't being pushed on them by their schools or government, so there is no control factor. I know the answer rests more on faith than science, but if nothing else, their circumstances contradict the logic that all Christianity is just forced on people. Much like its infancy, Christianity still remains a choice in the midst of overwhelming odds in several parts of the world.

Is it really possible that people could believe blindly and purposelessly in something for thousands of years? Why would so many millions of people, over such a long period of time feel the need to die (or kill) for something that was verifiably unreal? I'll give you a couple hundred naïve types that follow along with whatever they're told, but a couple hundred million? That seems like a stretch, and if science or history had a 100% method of disproving Christ, why hasn't it happened? Even Evolutionism doesn't "disprove" God. It simply disputes the manner in which we came into existence. Let's be clear, I'm not implying that because so many other people believe that you should too. Since you are reading this it tells me you are a person interested in learning for yourself, and not just following blindly. You want to know personally, not secondhand, and that is exactly what the bible calls for, a personal account.

According the bible, Christ didn't exist to support or reject science. He didn't come to earth to erase or eliminate other religions. And He sure didn't come to cause wars and fighting. Christ came for everyone that was interested to have a personal relationship with Him. For some that relationship may be about embodying His philosophies of love and peace. For others that relationship with Christ may be about putting Him in line with the many other religious entities that have existed throughout history. But for a specific few, that relationship entails so much more. *It's about Christ being our personal Lord and Savior. It's about serving and spreading His words. It's about representing Him in a fashion that welcomes others, rather than offending them. No matter what level anyone chooses, if any at all, it all starts with personal research. Read the New Testament of the bible for yourself and learn about Christ directly.* There may be things you don't understand 100% about the bible, but that doesn't make it less real. I don't know Trigonometry that well, but that doesn't mean math books are fake. But maybe if I took the time to study the subject, I may just learn something useful. It is no different with studying the bible.

Whether you decide to believe in a supernatural Christ or not, there are very few who can argue about the biblical principles of love, forgiveness, patience, perseverance, and numerous other attributes that we can all benefit from as individuals and as communities. #UniversalGood

Start with an open mind to the basics. Forget all the religious debates and biblical conundrums – for now. I'm not suggesting you never search out a deeper truth, just that you start with a solid understanding first. You can talk/argue religion for an entire lifetime and then some, and still not end up any better off. That is why this book is steering clear of that approach. Still, many of those conversations/arguments lack one essential element, someone who has actually read the material for themselves. Maybe understanding who Christ was and the stark differences between His values opposed to the religious leaders of the time, may just help you understand why Christians are so adamant about following Him, and how perfection is far from our resume! Keep an open mind and open eyes, don't get caught **squinting**.

Squinting – judging Christianity by what some people say or do, rather than what the bible explains. Generalizing all Christians into the same group based on limited personal experience.

Now of course, if I am wrong, and none of that is what you wanted to discuss, all I can say is, "oops." Maybe you have read the bible and it didn't make sense, or maybe it made perfect sense and you just don't believe it; just know that is completely your decision to make. The bible is very clear that not everyone will follow Christ, and that everyone has free will not to. If God allows it, why shouldn't we? So on behalf of all Christians that have ever lived and half way understood the bible the way it was supposed to be understood, then I apologize for the shortsighted behaviors of my Christian brothers and sisters that not only offended you, but violated the very words God instructed us to follow. Just know that God will judge them the same way they judge others, and you are free to believe or not to believe as you choose. But keep in mind that even modern science is researching the effects of faith and whether the brain alone can be solely responsible for consciousness. So science may soon be more of an ally for Christ. But Christian or not, feel free to keep reading and understanding the ins and outs of all the levels a little better, including some of the questions we didn't address in this section, like why God flooded the earth, allowed cities to be destroyed, and all the tragedies and unfortunate situations that still happen to this day. If you do decided to explore Christ, just remember it has to come from you directly. It shouldn't be your friends, and it sure can't be your parents.

NOTES:

TRADITIONAL
My parents are but....

This is the case for a lot of people. You have grown up in a house where your parents or guardians profess to be Christians (on some level), so praying, going to church, and talking about Christ, etc., are all things you can remember seeing or doing from the earliest age, including some religious cartoons or toys that were unfortunately never quite as cool as the mainstream stuff. So Christianity was just the norm, and has always happened without much thought or question. Let's be clear though, just because your parents are Christians, doesn't automatically make you one. When you are a toddler or young child, the bible says your parent's faith can cover you. I'm sure it has something to do with needing to dedicate all your time to potty training or shaping *Play-Doh*. **But once you get older and are capable of making your own mature decisions, you have to choose whether you want to understand who Christ is and if you want to have your own personal relationship with Him that doesn't require your parent's authority**. Sure, they may be able to instruct you to read your bible, or pray, or go to church, but realistically, no one can force you to be a Christian. There are plenty of individuals who perform Christian acts because their parents or an environment such as school, require them to do so, but:

Accepting Christ, repenting of sins, and living according to the bible is something that has to come from the heart, not from the presiding authority.

This level may be the most challenging of all the levels discussed in this book, because if you don't really understand Christianity or are interested in exploring other parts of life, you may feel trapped or conflicted to act like a Christian for your parents/guardian sake.
After all, despite whatever disagreements and arguments you may have, there is that strong sense of obligation to them since they are usually the ones who changed countless diapers, kept a roof over your head, food on the table, and provided for you most of your life (as I'm sure they remind you endlessly during those disagreements). Some of you may just pretend to go along with it so you don't hurt their feelings.

Some of you may even feel forced (or may actually be forced) into the religion because your parents are demanding you be involved. #Handcuffed

In worst case scenarios, punishment or consequences may happen if you don't participate. Just know that God knows your heart. Your parents may be content, but God knows if you are genuine or not in your beliefs, and He prefers the real deal.
You may listen to your parents or church leaders and feel Christianity has too many rules and limitations, or that people (possibly even your parents) are hypocrites because they do certain things that don't seem to be Christian. This may make you think twice about whether you want to be a Christian. What is important to understand is that all Christians have flaws and imperfections, even parents (shocking, I know). **Truthfully, even the greatest pastors and religious leaders have faults.** We just don't live under the same roof as them, like with our parents, so we aren't aware of what those others are doing on a daily basis. But you better believe everyone has their fair share of sins and challenges they are dealing with, just like your parents.

Only being around your parents so often probably makes issues seem more magnified because it's constantly in front of you. Truth is, even some of the greatest, most popular people in the bible were filled with flaws too. It's something we as humans can't escape.

In large, it doesn't really matter what your parents do. They could be the best Christians or the worst, none of that means anything in terms of *your* salvation, because when it's all said and done, Christianity is about your personal relationship and love for Christ. Personal. Not your parents, friends, teachers, co-workers, cousins, nobody can influence the degree to which you choose to accept Christ into your life. Maybe you just want to read the bible for wisdom or enlightenment? Maybe you want to get saved and not do any additional work like go to church or volunteer to help? Or maybe you might aspire to be the brightest, most dedicated Christian since the Apostles? All these scenarios are very feasible, and for the record, none of them are wrong. God gave you free will, use it how you choose. BUT, understand that being saved means a personal relationship with Christ, so all the time worried about what others are doing right or wrong, doesn't benefit or hinder you in the least.

Think of any relationship. Marriage, boyfriend and girlfriend, friends– what makes it work? Well, first, both sides need to be actively engaged and attempting to make it as great as possible.

<u>Then love, communication, trust, and time together are at the core of any successful relationship.</u> #StrongFoundation

It is no different with Christ. He's no longer here physically for us to sit down and have Starbucks with, but he still wants to spend time with us, spiritually! *But how do I connect spiritually with someone I can't see or Instagram? Isn't that like… a ghost?*

I'll admit, it's not as easy as it sounds. It's a difficult transition going from the sensual (touch, taste, smell, hear, see) world that we live in to a spiritual focus. From the time most of us are infants, we are comforted by being held, kissed for affection, tickled, spun around for play, and nurtured in physical affection.

Most of us, if we're fortunate, are taught to pray to God, but that's usually the extent of it. And truthfully, praying is just the beginning. So how do we build a relationship with a God we can't see? Well, by using the same characteristics that were mentioned above as foundational pieces of a healthy relationship (love, communication, trust, and time). Sure, those aren't the only things, but they are amongst the most critical. So let's take a look at each of those 4, to get a better understanding how utilizing them will help achieve a deeper spiritual connection with God.

Really these core components work together to strengthen each other, so it's difficult to label one more important than the other. Instead, we'll look at them in the order they usually evolve, starting with communication. No relationship has ever started without some type of communication happening first. It may have been face to face somewhere, online, through mutual friends, a letter, a text, it may have been a video, or even just simple eye contact, but no matter if it was verbal or nonverbal communication, an introduction was made and casual conversation ensued. People can't get to know each other and eventually spend time together without some form of communication. And no one can truly love or trust someone they've never communicated with. Even in absolute worst case scenarios like, say, MTV's Catfish, they may claim to be in love even though they have never met, but that was after they spent time communicating online first, even if it was fake.

So how do we communicate with God? He obviously isn't tweeting or updating a FaceBook status. If most of the cell phone service providers already have difficulties keeping a signal across an entire city, I'm pretty sure they would have a challenge supporting God's universal reach from Heaven. So what do we do? Well the easy, common answer is: prayer.

Many of us have been praying before meals and bed since we could first speak, so prayer is something almost everyone has done at some point in life. But unlike most definitions, prayer should be more than just a quick thanks or wish list of things we want from God.

It is true that we can use prayer to petition God for stuff we want. The bible says we can ask Him for things in Jesus name (John 14:13,14). But prayer should be much more than that. **Prayer is an opportunity to connect with God.** You can talk to him about your day, challenges you may be facing, accomplishments you have achieved. You can talk to him about your fears, or you can give thanks for things you have prayed for that came true. And maybe most importantly, you can talk to him about your unique purpose in life. Or you can even ask him questions. God how do I know you're there? Why did you allow ___ to happen? *But what good does it do to ask questions from somebody who won't talk back?* Oh, God will talk back! In fact, another popular form of Christian communication with God is the bible. *But the bible is just a book! It's not communication.* Actually, the bible is a form of communication. It is God's message to us about the history of Christianity and the principles we need to embrace to be better Christians.

Funny, if you ask people what are the keys to effective communication, most will come up with an extensive list: speaking clearly, thinking about what you want to say first, not interrupting the other person, etc., before ever mentioning the real key to communication – listening.

God gave us 2 ears and one mouth. Doesn't that mean we should be doing twice as much listening as talking? #QuietPlease

Listening is the foundation for healthy communication in any part of life, not just religion.

Without understanding the perspective of the person you're trying to communicate with, it will be tough to know what to say and how to say it, display your understanding, find common ground, address concerns, encourage them to support you, or even develop the other 3 traits of: love, trust and time. Well, the bible is the epicenter of listening to understand God and his ways. Reading and studying it daily exposes us to God's love, power, mercy, and grace, which usually sounds pretty appealing and makes us want to spend more time with Him, because it's not like the conditional or dysfunctional love we often experience with people. With God love is pure and perfect. The more time we spend understanding God's love and mercy, the more we learn to trust Him in faith. When our faith is strengthened, our communication with God becomes confident, because faith allows Him to increase His personal communication with us through his Holy Spirit (God's messenger). Soon we can begin to feel His presence and hear His voice within us, we see Him blessing us in life, which gives us even more motivation to continue learning and growing in Him. Sound kind of mushy? Only until you see how true it is and how your life changes!

Nothing living grows without some measure of time. Whether it takes decades like giant redwood trees or simply days like some small insects, some measure of time has to elapse. Growing in God is no different. We must take time to read and meditate on His word to understand what He wants from us as Christians. We must take the time to thank Him for all He has done and will do. Take time to understand how great and powerful He truly is.

We must pray for the needs of others and ourselves. Taking time away from busy days to listen to how He speaks to our spirits. We must take time to fellowship with others that are also growing, so we can share testimonies and learn through conversation and church. The more time we spend learning about God, the more we comprehend how much He really loves us and wants nothing but the best for us.

So much so that He sent his son, Jesus, to die for our sins and give us abundant life. And hopefully, this encourages us to seek Him out even more, because He always has more for us.

#IsGodOnYourCalendar?

When you spend a lot of time with someone who routinely shows you they have nothing but your best interest at heart, it becomes hard not to put some level of trust in them. Many of us can barely even trust ourselves 100% of the time because of mistakes from the past or bad habits we're aware of, but when you spend time reading about Jesus Christ, and how much He was willing to sacrifice for our benefit, He definitely earns at least a slight degree of trust, even from the most pessimistic of minds. Think about all the people throughout history who have been willing to fight and wage war in the name of, well, whatever cause was relevant at that moment. Money, power, revenge, love– you might want to get a bigger pen and extra paper because that is going to be a long list.

Now, when you finish, or your hand just feels like it's going to fall off from writing so much, think of all the people who have ever sacrificed their life, instead of fighting, for a cause they believed in. Of those people, were their causes for themselves, a select group, or all of mankind? Did they have enough followers that they could have waged war if they really wanted to, but chose not to? Did they also perform unheard of miracles that people still debate 2,000 years later?

Point being, yes there are some who risked their lives for worthy and noble causes for the benefit of others, but Jesus is in a class by himself, historically and spiritually. He did it for all of mankind, when He really didn't have to.

So just like people in any physical relationship slowly invest their trust in people who show them: 1) they want what's best for them 2) they want them to know and live in peace and truth, that's why Christians put their trust in Jesus. The more time we spend communicating with Him and seeing His truth become reality in our lives, then peace and blessings follow.

But trust doesn't always come easy. Sometimes we are hurt, let down, and disappointed by others, so it can become difficult to trust. Sometimes we keep our guard up so high and our heart so protected, that it almost seems impossible to trust. That's fine. No matter how many layers of emotional steel you have protecting your heart, God still knows what's on the inside. **If you commit to learning and practicing His word, in time you will see that you can trust Him with your heart.** When unexpected blessings or miracles happen, when potential catastrophes are averted, when successes flow, or even when there is just enough light to lead you out of some very dark places, it becomes increasingly more difficult not to trust in God.

Inevitably, if you communicate with someone regularly, spend time together, and have a trusting relationship, love will begin to blossom. In some cases it may be romantic love like with a boyfriend or girlfriend. In other instances it may be a platonic love like for a good friend. Then there is always the deep love that we have for parents and family members. But love relating to God is entirely different.

The bible tells us that He first loved us (1 John 4:19) before we even knew He existed. #KnowGreaterLove

---

29

So even though you may have been doing your own thing, acting crazy, getting into trouble, even though you may not have even been a Christian, God still loved you first. That is a love very few humans ever get to experience, because it is genuine unconditional love.

People are funny. One minute they love you to death, but the minute you do something they don't like, they never want to speak to you again. That's not the case with God. **Even though we may do things He doesn't approve of, His unconditional love for us won't allow His feelings toward us to ever change**. So no matter how much good or bad we do, He can't love us any more or less than He already does, which is infinite!

If acceptance of Christ sacrifice is what gives us salvation, then it is acceptance and reciprocation of God's love that builds the strong bond with Him. That is why at this point in life your parents can give you a whole lot of things, clothes, shoes, gadgets, etc., but they can't give or let you borrow their salvation and relationship with God. You must create and build your own. Again, the principles are no different than any other relationship. You couldn't ask your parents to love your boyfriend or girlfriend on your behalf. Why? Because that isn't their relationship! They may care about the person or love that you are with the person (maybe), but because they have an entirely different connection, only you can provide the necessary elements to make that relationship work for the two of you. It's the same with God.

If you decide to begin or strengthen your personal relationship with God, then you are taking a step of maturity. The bible gives the spiritual analogy that when you are a baby all you need is milk to sustain your body, but as you get older, you begin to need meat and more solid foods (Hebrews 5:12). When you are young the knowledge of God that your parents give you is enough for your age, but as you get older, it's imperative that you get more substance. Studying and learning about God must go beyond the Sunday School information you got as a child. That was great for laying a foundation, but now comes the real building, and that can be a little intimidating.

Whether it is the time away from friends, cancelling other engagements, the fear of being outcast or ridiculed by non-Christians, unbelief, the concern of not being able to live up to Christian standards, or any number of reasons/excuses people can come up with to remain status quo with their spiritual growth, you have to work past it. Any honest Christian will tell you, it isn't easy. But that doesn't mean it has to be a daunting task either. The truth is that it can be as difficult or as simple as you make it, and you can take it as far as the mind can imagine.

Most people don't discuss imagination when it comes to spirituality. Typically you'll hear knowledge, understanding, faith, belief, but rarely do you hear imagination. Well today we are introducing the topic, because it is as vital a necessity as almost anything else when it comes to your spiritual growth. We've already discussed (more than enough, I know) how your parents relationship with God is no longer sufficient for you to piggy back off of, so it is equally as important to understand that how God treats them, doesn't have to be how He treats you. In fact, God treats everybody different, because everybody has different levels of faith. As you probably know, faith is what we use since we can't physically see God standing in front of us, and the greater our faith, the more we can see and connect with God to unlock our potential, purpose, and blessings.

What does imagination have to do with faith?
#DreamBig

Well, if you think about faith as a fire, imagination is the air that helps expand the flames. It's not the fuel for the fire, because that would be the bible and books such as this that reveal God's truth.

Imagination wouldn't be the heat of the fire, because that would be the Holy Spirit that passionately connects us to God and encourages us on His behalf. So imagination would have to be the air that pushes the fire further and farther from where it originally started.

You see, there are many Christians who have a vast knowledge of God, but we all know that knowledge and imagination aren't the same things.

Knowledge is typically spoken of as information that we have stored up. But imagination? Not only can it be knowledge, but it can also stretch the boundaries of knowledge and create new knowledge! Think about the history of the telephone. Initially nobody had knowledge of the telephone because it didn't exist. They were content with speaking face-to-face or writing letters.

Then Alexander Gram Bell's **imagination** allowed him to apply his knowledge of communication and engineering to create the telephone and revolutionize the speed, distance and efficiency of communication around the world.

Within decades, almost everyone around the world had knowledge of the phone. Then people kept utilizing their imagination to refine it. The home phone with a direct call line so no operator was needed. The cordless phone so you weren't tied down to one location during your conversation. Call Waiting so you didn't get a busy signal when calling someone or miss an important call yourself. Then someone imagined the cell phone so you had a means to communicating when you were away from your home.

Then sometime later, Steve Jobs mixed his knowledge of the phone with his imagination, and created the iPhone, which was basically a mini-computer that makes phone calls.

And who knows what the future will hold when it comes to phones. Maybe just a small device that you place in your ear and it can read your mind of who you want to call and what you want to say.

The only limitations are a limited imagination. See how imagination plays such a key part of growth? Most people had knowledge of phones, they just didn't have the imagination to take it a step farther.

Faith is very similar, there are no boundaries. The bible says that all things are possible through God (Matthew 19:26), and when you look at some of His miracles, it's hard to refute that truth.

Except **many people don't let their imagination roam free when it comes to all the infinite capabilities of God, so they end up limiting their faith to what they know, rather than what could be**. But you have a distinct advantage over everybody when it comes to imagination and faith - you're still young! I know everybody can't wait to be 18 (or 21) so they can officially be treated like an adult, but I'm here to tell you, a lot of adults have some pretty heavy baggage that anchors down and even sinks their imagination. Maybe they have been rejected or terminated from several jobs so now they are pessimistic. Maybe they had children and feel they no longer have time to pursue their career ambitions, so they feel they have settled. Maybe they prayed about some things that didn't come to pass, so now their faith is limited. Maybe they have a bunch of bills and are stressing how they are going to make ends meet. If you didn't know already, these scenarios should give you a pretty good clue how the real world kicks in with some adults, and it's no longer about imagination and creativity. For many, it becomes more about working every day to get by and less about imagination and faith. For several, their faith in God isn't much bigger than the obstacles in their life, so they are always stuck facing the same challenges.

But hopefully since you're younger, you don't and won't have many of these problems. Hopefully you're still in a position where your imagination is working overtime about your future, and the sky is the limit. Believe it or not, that's exactly what God wants from you!

God wants you to imagine big, and then go to Him with the expectation that through your faith, He will make it happen. God wants big dreamers and thinkers. He likes blessing people on such a high level that everyone knows He had to be involved.

Think about when Jesus walked on water. Why did He do it? He could have limited his faith and just walked on land. He could have limited His faith and just believed that God would give Him enough strength to paddle a boat. But instead He applied His imagination to His faith and walked on the water, and the disciples immediately knew that God had to be involved. God doesn't want us to be tied down to tradition or norms. He wants us to serve Him with the creativity He has blessed us with. Sure, He wants us to stand firm on His word since his truth never changes, but He also wants us to think outside the worldly box on how we can use our talents for Him. And there are no limits. As far as space stretches, is as far as you can apply your imagination! Jesus never let his imagination and faith become restricted by what others told him. He always remembered that the bolder He was, the more glory it brought to God.

God wants the same thing today. He wants everyone to know that He is a part of your life, not just an extension from your parents. **He wants you to imagine all the things you can accomplish with Him through faith, so people will have no doubt that He blesses those who make it a point to trust, love, communicate and spend time with Him regularly**. But it all starts with your own personal relationship with Him. If you decide that you don't want to be under your parents umbrella when it comes to being saved and having a relationship with God, and you want to explore it on your own, then all you have to do is say this short prayer: "Jesus, I know you are the son of God and that you died and rose again for my sins. I ask that you forgive me today and come into my life as my Lord and Savior, so that I may have a new life in you. Amen"

It's really that simple. Sure there is a lot to learn and do as you continue to grow, but asking Christ to forgive your sins and accepting salvation through His sacrifice is all it takes to get the ball rolling.

<u>Who knows, your faith may cause you to be more blessed than your parents, grandparents, aunts, uncles, siblings and grandparents all put together!</u> But as a good Christian you would probably want to share with them, at least a little bit. The point is, **the only limits to God's grace and blessings in your life, are the ones you create through doubt and disbelief**. So spend time with God. Learn to communicate with Him and feel His presence. Develop your trust in Him, and love Him like you would love any person. In fact, make your love for Him, higher than your love for anyone else. Don't become so much of a fanatic where you can't relate to other people, just remember to keep your relationship with God as the top priority in your life. And as He reveals more of His power to you, may your faith spread farther than the farthest star so that everyone can see God distinctly at work in your life. And If you still aren't sure if you want to be a Christian or not, then take some time and research areas you may not be familiar with. Check it out for yourself.

NOTES:

EXPLORER

I'm checking it out

Ah, nothing better than the smell of fresh knowledge! So you're "checking out" Christianity to see what it's really all about. That's cool. Whether you have no prior knowledge or you fancy yourself the, spiritual yet non-religious type, there is nothing foolish about being knowledgeable. But before we get started, I do want to set one simple ground rule for this category, to be included you must be, kind of, slightly, actually – checking Christianity out. I know that may seem obvious, but I think there are more than a few people who claim to be researching religion or studying Christianity, and are really just expecting some spiritual lightning bolt to strike them. So for the record, random philosophical conversations on religion – do not qualify for this group. I'm not opposed to healthy, engaging conversation on spirituality. I'd definitely rather hear more discussion about God than some of these nonsense reality shows! But the problem is that in conversations, most people are only speaking from personal experiences. And **though Christianity is all about personal experience with God, there are some pretty well-defined cornerstones in the bible that aren't as open to interpretation.**

Think of someone who has never flown a plane before. There are hundreds of different aircrafts out there, from lightning fast fighter jets to huge cargo planes. Some cockpits are so massive they take multiple people to fly; while others are so small they can't fit more than one person. Someone who has never studied or flown before can't just engage into a discussion about the technicalities of flying (especially with actual pilots), and he really can't just jump in the cockpit of a plane and say, "I think I'm going to fly the plane this way!"

Well he could, but I'm positive no one would buy a plane ticket for that journey.

No, first he has to study the physics of flight, learn the instruments and dynamics of a beginner plane, then log some flight hours with a trainer to increase his knowledge of how that plane flies, and eventually fly solo and obtain his piloting license. Once he has done all that, then he may be a little more capable of having a meaningful conversation with other pilots. Yes, there are numerous similarities about planes, but without any type of background or actual learning, it is much too complex to just assume you know.

Christianity is often the same way. Many people want to talk about their opinions of Christ (including Christians), when the truth is that they have never really studied (or even read) the bible or sought to understand Christ. They want to talk, talk, talk, but there is no real substance to their words because they have no real foundation. Some of those people will speak from personal experience. "I went to a church and none of the people were friendly. So I don't like Christianity because the people aren't friendly." Or, "All the Christians I know are hypocrites, so I'll never be a Christian." That's what you would call, **squinting.**

Squinting – judging Christianity by what some people say or do, rather than what the bible explains. Generalizing all Christians into the same group based on limited personal experience.

The first thing to understand is, our personal experiences may be the cornerstone for our lives, but they are just a tiny fraction of all the reality that exists. So what if all the people at one church are mean. There are millions of churches across the world and I'm pretty sure not all of them are mean. Yes, some Christians are hypocrites. But who cares? A) Most religions are based on a doctrine, not people's actions,

and B) your spirituality is about you, not others!
Which basically means you must know the truth so you don't
fall into the same traps as the other hypocrites.

The truth is, checking out Christianity means dissecting
the message of the bible and other professional resources that
clearly explain what God intended Christianity to be, not what
people make it into.

Think of it this way. Have you ever known someone
who was really bad at a sport? I'm talking no athletic ability
whatsoever. Well, do you rate the sport based on that person
and say, this sport must not be any good because they aren't
any good. Or what about someone who can't sing to save their
life? Do you say, all music must be bad because they can't
sing? Yeah right! You look at their talent, or should we say
lack of, and compare it to professional athletes and musicians,
or people that exemplify, since they are the best in the world.
You realize as bad as the other person is, they aren't a good
measuring stick for what the sport or song is supposed to be.
It's no different with Christianity. **People, including myself,
will never be good models of how Christians should act.
We're all human so we all have our flaws**. That's why, if you
truly want to learn what Christianity is supposed to be, you
must turn to the bible and approved biblical resources that
teach with no bias. Get a direct account of Jesus Christ, and
how He exemplified what all of us imperfect people are
striving to be. He is the prototype of Christianity because He
is, well, the first six letters of Christianity. Then, after
strengthening your position and understanding, you're ready
for those random philosophical conversations.

#Don'tExpectPerfection

Wow. That was one exhausting definition, but now that we are hopefully in agreement with what this category consists of, let's get on to the next question, what exactly are you, 'exploring?'

If God is so good, how come He allows bad things to happen? How come there is such a big difference between the Old and New Testament in the bible? How do we know the bible is even real? How come every religion says all other religions are going to hell? How can God and Jesus be the same if Jesus called God, Father? What exactly is the Holy Spirit? Should I keep going? How many more questions can I list? There are infinite questions you can ask as you research Christianity. Some of you may have been exposed to Christianity so you are pretty familiar with the basics, others may have never heard any details whatsoever. It is okay wherever you are at, because we are all on our own spiritual journey. To be honest, many Christians have not only asked those same questions during their walk, but some still do. They are all valid questions that everyone should have some understanding of, and there are still many more that could be added. One thing to remember about Christianity though, no person knows everything (no matter how much they act like they do).

God is much too grand for our minds to completely understand him. #BeyondBoundaries

Think about it, the bible is just a fraction of God revealing himself to us, and we still don't even fully comprehend that much. Imagine if He showed us everything? Our brains would probably melt from information overload! But just because we can't grasp everything, doesn't mean we don't understand any at all. So let's look at a few of the more pronounced questions.

How am I supposed to follow a god that is supposedly so loving but allows bad things to happen to people? The answer is, you're not. The God we speak about in Christianity isn't to blame for the many travesties and terrors that happen around the globe, we are! See, God is the absolute truth. He can't tell a lie, or even a partial truth.

We can all remember those days when we would get into some kind of situation and our parents would say, tell me the whole truth. They knew as kids we were likely to leave out a few details (usually the incriminating ones) that might get us into trouble. We hear the same thing in the courtrooms on TV. "Do you promise to tell the whole truth, nothing but the truth, so help you God?" Yet, somehow, both sides still have completely contrasting stories. Both can't be right.

It's just an undeniable fact of life that people lie. But not God! The truth is formed around His words and promises. So when He gave mankind free will, it meant He would no longer force us to do one thing or another. He can't say, I'm giving you free will, but I'm not going to allow you to kill, steal or do anything bad. Then it wouldn't be free will, it would be partial will. **God gave us free will to do pretty much whatever we want.** So when we witness bad things happen, it's usually the result of someone's freedom to decide to do bad instead of good.

Now, that doesn't mean God doesn't care or attempt to stop people from doing wrong. He is constantly reaching out to people with simple laws and guidelines (i.e. Thou shalt not kill. Thou shalt not steal) to more complex moral characteristics (love, patience, forgiveness). But those things are written in the bible for people to read and follow- or not. But the bible is God's way of saying, if you would only follow these words, your societies and world would be free of all the wars, murder, theft, rape, abuse, etc.

In fact, God doesn't stop there, He sends his Holy Spirit (think: the voice of god) to whisper His preferences of the positive things we should do, especially before we make a bad decision without considering potential backlash.

In fact, some people ask why God gets mad if we have free will but don't use it to follow what He wants. It's not that He is mad, just disappointed. He knows when people choose not to listen or obey, they have to live with the consequences, and sometimes those consequences affect us all. But again, He won't force us to do anything. <u>He will only guide our lives if our freedom of choice is to have the faith to follow Him</u>. By the way, He isn't just letting bad things happen, He will judge everyone based on the lives they chose to lead – rights and wrongs.

How do we know that the bible is real? This question was posed an answered in the, "I'm Not" chapter, but there is another related question we can tackle, how can the bible be real if it is so full of contradictions?

To say that the bible is complicated is like saying the ocean is deep or that space is vast. But what the bible should never be is intimidating or confusing. God didn't design it to scare people away. In fact, it is just the opposite. **God wants those who choose to become Christians, to understand exactly why they are following Christ.** You can think of the bible as a user's manual. It covers everything from the creation of the universe to sexual morality. It tells of the history of Christianity, including the development of Judaism and many centuries later the life of Jesus and those that would continue His message. The bible gives us world prophecy, personal guidance, loads of insight, and assurance in what we cannot always see. B.I.B.L.E - Basic Instructions Before Leaving Earth is an acronym some have used. But no matter what, the bible is a representation of who God is.

But some people say the bible contradicts itself. There were even times when I used to wonder how one scripture could say one thing, and another seemed to be opposite.

Or how Jesus could say things like, "turn the other cheek," but the Old Testament is filled with wars in God's name.

At a glance, there are a few areas that seem to suggest inconsistency, but despite what critics may suggest, the bible goes together just as God intended. Since this is the *researching* chapter, let's take a look at some of the legitimate reasons why the bible is so misunderstood.

1) Context – Whether a person has an ulterior motive to try and discredit the bible or just innocently plays bible roulette (randomly flips to a page/scripture), many people do not study the bible in its entirety. I've seen people argue against Christianity so passionately they will take go into full **page rage**. Page Rage - Taking one excerpt from the bible to justify a point, and completely ignoring every word before and after. The problem isn't religious, anything taken out of context is probably going to be misinterpreted, and the bible is no exception. Understanding how it all gels together from beginning to end is necessity if you want to get it.

2) Translation – The bible was originally written in Hebrew. Then some time later it was translated into Greek, and then King James (yes, that guy who has his name on several bible covers) had it converted into Latin, before it made its way around the world in practically every language imaginable. The issue with translation isn't about which one is more right, it's about accuracy. Some words can take on a different meaning or connotation in a different language. Other words may not translate at all. So definition is something that has to be taken into account, especially during the confusing parts.

3) Experience – How much experience does the person reading or assessing the bible have? Is this their first time reading it? Have they ever read the whole thing? Have they taken bible study classes? Are they what could be considered an expert? This is a big deal. You wouldn't let someone with no medical experience perform brain surgery on you. You wouldn't let someone with no financial experience invest your money. So why do we let people with no experience influence our understanding of the bible? I'm not saying people aren't entitled to their opinion, but just because we have opinions doesn't mean they are facts. It is best to read a study bible that has been verified or speak to a scholar with specific questions to get truth, not feelings.

4) Interpretation – Inevitably after you add context concerns to translation tie-ups to random personal experience, the result is an interpretation. It may be a terrible interpretation, it may be exactly what God intended, or it may be a general acceptance or agreement at face value, but there will be an interpretation of some sorts. In the introduction we joked about the many denominations of Christianity, where do you think they all came from? If you guessed, various interpretations of the bible, then this book is either really doing its job helping you understand Christianity, or you were already pretty smart to begin with. I think it's a combination of both!

5)   Personal preference – At the end of the day, people are people, and believe it or not, aside from spaceships and smart phones, we haven't changed much from the biblical days in terms of character. We have been divided since Cain and Able, and we still are today. The bible even discusses how some of the disciples disputed over which leaders to follow. The truth is, for many people, personal preference takes priority. Often times it doesn't matter who's really right or wrong, it's about their feelings. It's about preference. Which is why many people that debate whether the bible is real, or contradicts itself, will never change their mind. <u>They aren't looking for God's truth, they are looking to validate their own truth.</u> And Christians aren't immune to this either. We're human too. Just know that real Christianity sometimes involves sacrificing our own personal preference, and accepting God's preference over our thoughts and actions. He who loses his life will gain it!

Regarding the stark contrasts between the Old Testament and the New Testament, We could exhaust that conversation in a book all too itself, and some actually have. So it probably best to go with the simple explanation of a few items.

A)   We must remember there is a way that God wanted us to be, i.e. Jesus Christ in the New Testament, and there is the way we ended up, The Old Testament. It's not that God wanted His people to do some things like go to war, but if they didn't fight they could have been decimated by a pagan worshipping civilization, which would suggest their false God was more powerful than the real God (remember - free will. People could choose to worship other gods or even kill. So God frequently intervened on behalf of those who chose to worship Him. Seem unfair? It is! But that's what happens when you bow down to a gold cow instead of the Creator of the universe). During that time, people worshipped all kinds of different God's and religions, and many of those territories far outnumbered the Hebrew people. So when Abraham or David won those miraculous battles, if gave truth to God's real power versus the demonic influence of the pagan gods.

B)   God didn't want to create 600+ rules (Yeah, in case you didn't know the 10 commandments barely scratched the stone tablet surface) for Moses and the Israelites when they were in the desert after escaping slavery and the harsh rule of Pharaoh. But they had been so brainwashed by Egyptian mythology over the 400 years they were captive, the commandments God gave were meant to be a meticulous way to keep them thinking about God and break out of the pagan ways they had inherited while in Egypt.

C)	To blame God for the bad things that happen is like blaming the judge for sentencing someone who is clearly guilty of a crime. We're not talking about a questionable case; this would be what attorneys' call a, "slam dunk." All the evidence lines up and the person has even admitted guilt. Whether we confess or not, we as people are guilty of the chaos in our world, not God. He gave us clear and concise guidelines to live a peaceful and prosperous life, if we choose not to follow them, then we are at fault. And because He did give us the perfect blueprint, we should trust that His judgments are always righteous.

Despite its complexities, the bible remains one of the most popular books on earth. Whether reading it to learn and grow, or reading to learn how to dispute it, just remember not to get caught in **Page Rage**. Both Christians and non-Christians are often found guilty of this in being more driven to prove their point than understand the whole truth.

Page Rage - stressing one page/excerpt/scripture from the bible, rather than keeping everything in context.

Here's another popular question for those checking out Christianity, why do all religions claim they are the only way to God, or that everyone else will burn in hell? I'm not the expert to speak on every religion, honestly if it wasn't for God working through me I wouldn't be able to write this book.

But when it comes to this question and Christianity, we must go back to a common theme you're probably tired of hearing me say, or I mean write, whatevs.

People's interpretation or opinion opposed to what the bible actually states. In the bible there is a scripture where Jesus says, "No man cometh unto the father but by me (John 14:6)." I think many people have perceived this to mean all kinds of things, but when we apply God's unconditional love, mercy and forgiveness, I think there is only one logical explanation.

When Christ says, cometh unto the father, I believe He is referring to being in the eternal presence of God, meaning heaven. I'm not advocating other religions, but I'm also not denouncing there may be several paths a person can take to, "recognize there is a God," while in this physical life on earth. Think about it, *people convert to Christianity from other religions all the time*. Some are born into a religion, others may not have had exposure to Christianity (at least in the real way), or may have just been confused or mislead.

That doesn't mean they didn't know that one supreme God existed. That doesn't mean they didn't love or commit to Him whole heartedly, it just means the truth of Christ hadn't been put into their hearts yet. But because they had a true desire to worship God, eventually He exposed them to the way, the truth and the life – Jesus Christ. Once they understood, they converted. And usually those that convert from other religions can be great spokesmen for Christ, because they are able to compare the principles of other religions that we as Christians may not be aware of. That is why it is so imperative Christians not be hateful or intolerant of others. **We can't forget that only God knows a person's heart and their future.**

We have no way of knowing what lessons another person is learning under a different religion. For all we know, a person of another religion may convert to Christianity and go back and help convert many others.

After all, it was Jewish people converting Gentiles that formed Christianity to begin with! Second, regardless of whether a person converts or not, we as Christians are commanded not to judge and to love our neighbors as ourselves.

The bible doesn't say, love your neighbor, as long as they are the same religion and are really easy to get a long with. It says, love. Period. I once saw a quote on a church billboard that said, "God appreciates a kind atheist more than a mean Christian." Think about it, which one of those two is actually acting more like Christ?

As far as who is going to heaven and who is going to hell, I don't think any of us can definitively say who will and who won't end up where. Some Christians will argue that the bible clearly says, the only way to get into heaven is to accept Jesus as your Lord and savior and to be baptized, and I'm not disputing the bible. I'm simply saying, I don't pretend to know who is and isn't saved, or know all of God's mysterious ways. I certainly don't give people information contrary to what the bible says about going to heaven, I just find that,

<u>if we as Christians spend more time demonstrating God's love in our actions and speech and focusing on the freedoms we have in Jesus, then we probably don't need to worry about delivering the, "damned to hell speeches" as much.</u>

God wants people to know He is a God of love and mercy first, punishment and consequences second. **#GodIsLove**.

That's why the new testament of the bible commands us to love more than any other instruction. But many Christians, maybe even some you know, tend to forget this. Not only do they forget their love to God, they neglect their love for others and sometimes even love for themselves. See, a lot of Christians get so entangled in the law of the bible, the, "do this and don't do that," rules, that love becomes an afterthought because they are so unrealistically focused on trying to reach an unreachable state of perfection.

Then as others, particularly people that are still learning about Christ, witness that attitude, they are likely to be turned off by unrealistic expectations that people have set, not God. Or they may feel they are not worthy of heaven because of people judging as if God appointed them jury, when we know that isn't the case. So who's getting into heaven and who's not? The only way to really know is focus on our own individual relationships and purpose with Christ and make sure we are there to see firsthand.

An interesting battle that has been waged in churches (and even schools and government settings), is the science versus religion debate. Though I'm not really sure what most of the debate is about, I thought I'd bring it up because supposedly it's a pretty big deal. The reality is, most of science and religion coexists just fine. Science is simply the, "study of," something.

For instance, God made rain for drinking water, farming, etc. It doesn't make His creation any less valuable because scientist study the process of how rain comes out of clouds. They are just deriving their information from elements that God produced. Simple. Another example, God created man and gave him cognitive thinking. Science, or more specifically - psychology, studies how the mind works in practical terms. It's not an, either or scenario. They both serve a purpose.

Now, I won't stand on complete naivety. Where there is a more intense debate, and more opposition from many Christians, is when it comes to evolution. And in this corner, Mr. Survival of the Fittest, Charles Darwin! His opponent, Mr. Survived after being dead 3 days, Jesus Christ! See, to spare decades of debate and hours worth of cliff notes, it basically boils down to the bible saying God created the universe and then man and all the animals in their adult form over a 7 day period. Whereas evolution holds the Big Bang Theory, the entire universe started from a gaseous explosion and a single celled organism created all life forms through the process of evolution.

Personally, if I were to step outside my Christian beliefs, I think one takes just as much faith to believe as the other. A giant invisible God or something as ginormous as the universe from nothing? I know without faith Christianity and the elements of the spiritual life can be difficult to grasp, but what evidence do scientist really have, other than theory, that is so much more compelling? It's not like they have a time machine that can take them back billions of years to verify.

I'm not saying life never evolves. We know it does. Man evolved from drawing crude pictures on cave walls to megapixel camera phones. We see animals evolve to adapt to their changing habitats. Evolution happens. But to say that a single cell organism could evolve to one day have the imagination and cognitive comprehension to engineer a cell phone that lets you surf the net while talking, without some sort of divine intervention?

Well to me that would be no greater of a curiosity than a man walking on water or feeding 5,000 people with a couple of fish sandwiches (shout out Pastor Ron Taylor)! But since I have experienced unexplainable personal blessings and relationship with God, faith in Him is the much more logical choice for me.

So what about those who don't have a first hand account with God and personal proof? How do they decide between the two? I honestly don't think they have to. Again, we as Christians can be so oppositional or argumentative, that we often don't even consider bigger possibilities. What if evolution didn't take billions of years, but it was the process God used to create the cosmos in the 7 days the bible references? Or, when the scripture says a thousand years is but a day to God, is it possible creation actually spanned over 7,000 years instead of 7 calendar days?

Not that God couldn't create the cosmos in 7 days. He could create a universe in 7 seconds if he wanted, but I don't think He cares about time as much as us because He is eternal.

I'm just saying, <u>when Christians are secure in their faith, many of those semantic arguments are pointless (unless your purpose involves a more analytical approach)</u>. I know God created everything! How He did it isn't my biggest concern. I'm not dancing around the debate of evolutionism versus creationism, I just happen to know there are numerous books and articles examining the two, and I'm not sure how many people have gotten saved because of them. If most Christians spent as much time demonstrating love as they did arguing issues that take either a) completely spirit filled insight or b) scholarly study, many of those who might be "checking out" Christianity would probably gravitate toward the warmth of us as people, not the miraculous transforming single cell.

#LoveOverLectures

Speaking of miracles, that is always a hot topic when it comes to the bible. People read the bible for all sorts of reasons. There are those who read the bible because of the entertaining stories, to learn the characteristics that Jesus embodied, to compare religious doctrine, to be motivated, build their faith, and yet many who read don't believe in any of the miracles or the supernatural element. Maybe it's just me, but I've always found it humorous that of all the things to challenge about God, miracles makes the list. So there is a spiritual being that created the universe, but cannot do anything beyond what the average person can do? I've watched TV shows that attempted to explain how miracles might have happened in scientific terms. For instance, Moses parting the Red Sea. One theory was that they crossed at a really shallow end, during a really low tide, while a strong wind separated the water and showed the path. Wow! That seems very…elaborate. And neglectful considering the bible mentions the water being deep enough for them to see fish and drown the Egyptian army.

The real problem with these, "rationalizations," is that life is full of unexplainable events and situations, so why is it so hard to believe that God couldn't be responsible? The biggest reason probably has to do with the fact that we are visual creatures. If I ask you what super powers Superman has, what would you say? He can fly. He can see through things. He's strong. I don't think one person would say, Superman doesn't have any super powers because he isn't real. We see him in movies, comics, etc. But we don't associate super powers like that with God because we can't see Him. So it is tough for us to imagine without a visual reference. Another reason might be because we don't see the same kind of miracles being performed today, so there is limited association. The miracles end up reading like more of a fairy tale than an example of God's greatness. But miracles were and continue to be real. They just need a mustard seed of faith to get going.

I also want to throw this last thing out there – don't let Christians turn you off from being Christian. It's there. I see it. Most people do. **Christians can be hypocritical and judgmental**. We aren't always the best example of why Christ is so worthy. The problem is that many Christians don't know how not to be hypocritical or judgmental. They don't know how to not generalize. They don't know how, because that's not something specific to Christians, that a problem for most people in society at large. *"Yeah, but Christians are supposed to be loving. They are supposed to embody a God that is forgiving and accepting. They don't act anything like the bible says. They're the biggest hypocrites in the world!"* Well, there's only one thing I can say to that. You're right. No Excuses. Just remember, everyone will have to answer to God for their work on earth. Don't let others discourage you.

Focus on learning the truth about Christ, not the truth about Christians. There is a pretty big difference! #TheReal

Remember, no matter how much you explore Christianity, there are some things you will never learn or know unless you are actually a Christian exercising your faith in God. He reveals more of himself to those who truly seek Him for personal relationship, not just because they want to. You can still learn a lot or the truth, but some can only be revealed in faith. There were times in the bible when the religious group who opposed Jesus, the Pharisees, demanded a sign or miracle from Him to prove that he was really the Messiah and Son of God. Jesus never did it. *But why not? Wouldn't that have been the easiest way to make everybody believe and end all the disputes? Couldn't God just show some grand miraculous sign now and prove He is real and end all of the wars and debates?* The answer then is the same answer now. Miracles and signs are happening all around us. Many Christians are living testimonies through their actions, insights and even past.

The truth is, if we want to know God is real, it must start with our hearts, not with our eyes. #Genuine

That's why Jesus never gave the Pharisees a sign. He was performing miracles everyday! Numerous healing miracles, raising people from the dead, walking on water, feeding of thousands, and too many to name right here, so why didn't the Pharisees see those? Their hearts were closed. They weren't trying to know if Christ was real because they wanted to glorify and worship him (which was technically their jobs), they were worried about their lifestyles being disrupted. How much money, power and prestige they might lose. They weren't in it for God's glory. Don't let Christians or anyone else fool you, God is perfectly okay with you researching, asking questions, and even speaking to Him directly about things you don't understand. Just remember, beyond all the books and advice, learning the whole truth about God at some point will take a leap of faith.

NOTES:

DISCIPLE
Saved and learning about Christ

CONGRATULATIONS! Whether you recently made the decision to accept Jesus Christ as your lord and savior or if it was something you did a while back, I'm sure it still feels good to know that you are redeemed by the blood of God's son. Just remember, the wonderful life that God has in store for you is a life long process. Since God's wisdom is so infinite, <u>all the ways that we can grow and flourish as Christians is literally limitless</u>. So the real question is no longer, are you saved, but what are you now learning about Christ and how are you applying it to your life?

One of the biggest, immediate lessons you learn after being saved is God's forgiveness. Sure we read about it everywhere in the bible, but it's only after we get saved that we truly feel and appreciate Christ's sacrifice for our sins. Sin. It is also a pretty big deal at this stage, because you may not have fully grasped that all your sins, no matter how bad you think they are, are still forgiven. You may understand that Christ died, but do you understand his resurrection and ascension? You may get that all your past sins are forgiven. In fact, if you're anything like me, when you first got saved you spent days crying and reflecting on all the negative things you have done over your lifetime and how it is almost unreal that Christ could forgive so much. But the real kicker, that you need to realize more and more as you grow, is that <u>when the bible says He died and rose again for all your sins, it even</u>

<u>meant your future ones</u>. Stuff you don't even know you're going to do has already been forgiven!

Since we're discussing sin, it probably helps to define it a little bit. We know that sin is something that goes against what God instructs. And that doesn't just mean things the bible talks about, He will instruct you personally in some areas too. That means you generally have two types of sin: **1) Omission and 2) Commission**. A sin of commission is one you directly *commit*. For example, stealing a pack of gum from the store is a sin of commission. You thought about it and you did it. On the flip side, a sin of omission is something you didn't do, but you should have, as in, *omitted*. So let's say that you didn't steal the gum, you paid for it. But instead of giving you one dollar back in change, the cashier accidentally gives you one hundred dollars back. You didn't ask for it. It wasn't your fault she made the mistake. But when you realize it, rather than returning it, you keep it. That is a sin of omission. As a Christian you should always strive to do what is right. Not doing something that you know should be done (omission), is as much of a sin as directly doing something that is wrong (commission). Neither is better or worse than the other, and fortunately, both are forgiven by Christ's blood. But that doesn't mean the enemy won't try to distract you with guilt when you do make a mistake.

Guilt has been and always will be one of the devil's greatest weapons. He'll tempt and tempt you, never giving up with his quest to make you sin or backslide. Many times you will be successful in avoiding his snares, other times, not so much. So what does the devil do as soon as he is done tempting you enough to make you slip up and sin? He throws it right back in your face! Here are some of the popular clichés you may hear the devil echo to you after you make a mistake. *"See, you're not ready to be Christian. You're still sinning." "How can God use you when you're still making mistakes like that?" "Who's gonna believe you're a Christian with you sinning like that? More like a hypocrite!"* "How many times do you expect God to *forgive you?" "You're better off not telling anybody you're a Christian that way they can't judge you."* Statements like those are what the devil will attack you with to try and separate you from God's forgiveness and love. Because the more he can use guilt to isolate you from God, the less likely you will do the things God wants you to do. **Fellowshipping with like-minded Christians, studying the bible, praying, fasting, praising and worshipping are five staples that should be a part of every Christians' daily routine.** They are all things that help us to grow in the spirit and fulfill our purpose. BUT...if the devil can make you feel guilty and forget that you are forgiven, then he can separate you from meeting those daily necessities and make you feel like you are on your own, maybe even push God away. Think about it, when you have done something wrong to a parent, teacher or friend, once you feel that guilt kick in don't you wish you could hide on the opposite end of the earth? It's the same with God. Guilt will cause you to slow down on the five essentials, or worse, stop completely! Then you begin to drift away from God, and the devil is successful in discouraging another future servant.

Many Christians never reach their full potential because they are so anchored in guilt from sins and mistakes. But every sin we will ever commit is forgiven! So cut the anchor and set sail. #BeFree!

You are forgiven by God, for every sin – past, present and future! Everything the devil tries to convince you of is a lie. In fact, all he can do is lie! He didn't earn the nickname, The Father of all Lies, for being honest. See, when you thought you got saved because you heard about Christ dying for your sins, you thought you were making a choice and everything was happening right then and there. But the truth is that God had been waiting for that moment since before your oldest ancestor. God knows everything. He knew that you would accept His offer of forgiveness and eternal salvation. He knew that you would want to learn and grow, and eventually become a servant (which we will talk about later) to help build His kingdom. But God also knew you weren't perfect, and that you never would be. That's why he sent Christ to compensate for all of our sins and flaws, so that <u>we never have to be perfect</u>. We push as hard as we can, and when we do mess up, whether it be 1 or 1 million times, we rest confidently that Christ has already forgiven us. In our walk with God we can expect a few stumbles. We make mistakes, God doesn't. He will always be there to help us back up, and continue to love us unconditionally. **So forgiveness is something we can expect, not worry or debate with the devil about.** Remember, God is omniscient. He knows everything that has or will ever happen in our personal lives, and He has made the offer to forgive us anyway! Our sins are not a factor!

Worrying about sin!

So if our sins don't matter, why can't we just do anything we want? There is a long and short answer to that. The short answer is because now that we have dedicated our lives to God, we want to do things that are pleasing to Him, and pleasing Him simply means knowing and doing what the bible teaches us. The apostle Paul talks about this at length.

Romans 6:13: Do not let any part of your body become an instrument of evil to serve sin. Instead, give yourselves completely to God, for you were dead, but now you have new life. So use your whole body as an instrument to do what is right for the glory of God.

The long answer isn't more complicated, it's just, well, longer. When we get saved it is initially for us, for our own eternal salvation. But as we demonstrate commitment and growth in God, it becomes more than just about us. It evolves into God revealing His purpose in our lives, so we can go about fulfilling our role in His kingdom. Discovering your purpose is already difficult enough, you don't need old sins that have been forgiven distracting you.

Getting past sin is essential to your walk in Christ. If you get hung up on your mistakes you will lose sight of the key to Christianity…it was God's grace through Christ's death and resurrection that saved us, not our works. You have to realize that your purpose and blessings will not change. Your sins don't take away from what God has for you any more than the good things you do add to it, because at the end of the day, it's not about what we do. Not your mistakes, or the mistakes of everyone combined can overshadow Christ's sacrifice. Everything, literally everything, I repeat everything (getting the point), everything is about God's grace and glory. If you forget this, you will fall into one of the devil's many traps that manipulate your pride (Too much pride brings arrogance, too little pride destroys confidence). There is never a circumstance when you aren't already forgiven by God. He is patient and loving on a level that we could never understand. We tend to associate the way God loves us with the way we love each other as people, and it's just not the same. He doesn't have a long, tiring day and take His frustrations out on us. He isn't holding grudges from things we did two years or even two days ago. God's forgiveness is like yesterday never existed, like it never happened. And that's how He treats our sins, like they never existed. Because of that forgiveness, we can continue on boldly, with the reason He created us. No sin should ever make you lose sight of your purpose.

God's purpose for you is far greater than your mistakes. #BigPicture

Your journey will be filled with numerous peaks and valleys, bumps and bruises, joy and pain. There will be times when your walk with God is tested. You may question if the entire bible is real. Why God allows some of the things He does. Your faith may, no, erase that, your faith will waver at times. Don't worry about any of this. God knows better than anyone that people have battled with cases of doubt from the beginning. The Israelites doubted God for forty years despite some of the most miraculous acts recorded in the bible! That's why Jesus told his disciples, "Because you have seen me, you have believed; blessed are those who have not seen and yet have believed (John 20:29)," He knows we are groomed in the old philosophy, "seeing is believing," and we don't get to see a fraction of the miracles they witnessed in the bible.

He is patient while we learn and digest Hebrews 11:1- faith is the substance of things hoped for, the evidence of things not seen. #GottaBelieve

There are a lot of things you will need to do to strengthen your faith. Bible study every day. This is a critical area of the Christian walk in order to understand the history of Christianity and God's ways. You'd be surprised how many Christians don't read the bible, which should leave no surprise how many Christians don't have a better knowledge of who God is and what He wants from us. There are different translations of the bible, so get one that works for you. If you don't like the Shakespeare style writing in the King James Version, try the NLT version and get one that includes a study guide to help grasp exactly what the scripture is saying. And don't worry if a little **BiQuil** kicks in.

BiQuil - When you try to read the bible at night and it puts you right to sleep. But, better to fall asleep with the Word than something crazy like before you got saved!

Some other daily staples include praying, praying and praying some more to always seek God's direction. There will always be gaps when we don't pray as much as we should or realize we have gone a while without thinking about God, but all we can do is try to cut down those big breaks and learn to keep moving God to the front of the priority list.

One way to accomplish this is through praise and worship. Praise and worship God regularly, constantly giving thanks with your words and actions. God deserves to be acknowledged for His greatness. Even if that means setting calendar appointments until it becomes a natural reaction. Fellowship with other Christians that are interested in growing like you. This includes a bible based church. Some think church is not a necessity to being saved, and technically they are right.

You can be saved without going to church. BUT, be careful. Not going to a church may hinder you from growing like you are supposed to. A good church not only provides solid fellowship, but a deeper understanding of the bible, which promotes faith!

Lastly, fasting, periods where you sacrifice a particular area in order to be more focused on God. Bible study, prayer, fasting, fellowship, and praise shouldn't be goals, think of them as responsibilities, as necessary as breathing.

When you practice all 5 of these pieces regularly, not only will they strengthen your faith, they will put you on the path to something much, much bigger. Discovering you purpose! There are many Christians who are saved who have yet to commit their actions to Christ, but for those that have dedicated their life, purpose is on the horizon.

Don't be scared when you hear the word – purpose. Some people immediately think, "No way! I'm not gonna be some monk or preacher!" Don't worry, that's usually not the case. First of all, if everyone had their own church, who would be left to attend and support? Where would we even find enough space to build all those churches? Second, even if everyone were called to be preachers, since not everyone actually discovers and fulfills their purpose, there would still only be so many that actually follow through. But the truth is, while some of you may discover you have a calling to preach, most of us will learn we have a distinct purpose in some other area of God's will. My purpose for instance, is to write books and work with young adults. Some people are talented musicians who glorify God and touch people's souls with music. Some are Christian bloggers who reach millions everyday with inspirational blogs. There are missionaries who travel the globe spreading the word. Some people don't need to travel that far, their purpose is to talk about Christ right in their own neighborhood. And still, other people's purpose may not be to talk about Christ at all. Some people are just meant to be good Christian representatives. Their friendly disposition or kind heart may be exactly what it takes for others to see a positive, non-aggressive side of Christianity.

The point is that everyone has a different purpose. And whether you are intended to reach one person or one billion, everyone's purpose is equally important. Who knows? You may reach one person that goes on to reach one billion. Never underestimate the value of your purpose. What is purpose and why is it important?

In a nutshell, it is the job God intended for you and only you to complete as a Christian. #UniqueYou

Everyone's purpose will be as unique as there are people walking the planet, but every purpose has the same goals, 1) glorify God 2) to build and strengthen God's kingdom 3) demonstrate God's unconditional love 4) get your blessings! Because God gives us free will and doesn't force anyone to do anything, it is Christians (working in God's love and spirit) that help unbelievers learn about Christ as well as encourage other believers to deepen their faith. It's not that God couldn't show the world some giant miracle to prove His existence if He wanted, but after Christ died for our sins, the ownership to spread His word is now on us through purpose. Remember, that's the nutshell of what and why purpose is important. The truth is, it is much more complicated than that. You may hear entertainers thanking god when they win awards, despite the fact that their work may be the exact opposite of what the bible talks about. Does that mean they *aren't* living their purpose? You may know people who act high and mighty like Christ calls them on their cell phone. But does that mean they *are* living their purpose? Maybe your purpose will be to clarify those questions to the rest of the world. Or maybe, since God will be the final judge, it is best to accept that we can't really stress whether others are living their purpose or not, because we will be busy enough trying to determine and live our own.

So how do you know what your purpose is? Unfortunately this book will not be able to tell you your specific purpose. BUT, before you run to get a refund, it can help guide you on the steps you need to take for God to reveal your purpose in due time. Hint, hint, yes, "due time," means it will require, amongst other things, some **PATIENCE** on your part. Sometimes it feels like we have to be doing something, and sometimes we do, but sometimes we need to stay still and wait on God.

Numbers 9:8 - And Moses said to them, "Stand still, that I may hear what the Lord will command concerning you."

Don't expect learning your purpose to be an overnight process. It took the disciples three years directly under Jesus to learn what they needed. They literally watched Him perform miracles, get crucified, rise from the dead, and then ascend into heaven, and they still had doubts and disagreements. The apostle Paul went blind for several days (Acts 9:9) after hearing God's voice before he understood his purpose, and he wrote most of the New Testament. Hopefully the following steps will help you live and learn your purpose, so you won't have to go through some of those extremes to play your part.

We've already mentioned patience, another quality you will have to demonstrate if you want God to show you your purpose is **COMMITMENT**. Commitment not only to your own growth, but you must also show commitment to serving God and others. Think of it like this. If you had a multi-million dollar company and had to promote one of your employees to run the operations, if all of their qualifications are equal, would you rather hire a person who has been committed to the company, or someone with an attitude like, whatevs? If you want your company to succeed, you hire the person committed to the job. God wants you to show a similar commitment. Oh, and it's not to prove anything to Him, it's to prove it to yourself. See, it's one thing to be responsible for yourself. It's a completely different story to be responsible for somebody else. Will you have the passion and persistence? Will you put the needs of others higher than yours? It's easy to say yes, but to follow through consistently takes focus. That's why you can start off small and work your way up. Volunteer on a church ministry. Get involved with a community organization that helps those in need. Be a teacher's assistant for a lower class level. These are all ideas to explore to show you are committed to serving others. Notice, none of these are paying jobs? There is nothing wrong with getting paid to help others, but it can be very difficult to separate whether your motivation is a paycheck or God's purpose, so usually volunteer work helps to avoid any confusion. UNDERSTAND, once you actually learn your purpose, there is nothing wrong with getting paid for it. God wants to bless you. Unpaid volunteer work is simply for showing you are willing to commit time and energy to others, without getting anything in return.

#WithLifeComesSacrifice.

SACRIFICE is something that we give up, in order to please God. It may be a sacrifice given directly to Him, like not watching your favorite TV show so you can spend more time in prayer, or not buying a new pair of sneakers so you can donate the money to kids who live in a homeless shelter. Sacrifice may be like fasting, where you give something up for a period of time in order to improve your spiritual focus. We see sacrifices in movies where someone gets pushed into a volcano or a man has to rescue some woman from being sacrificed by a gang of lunatics. In fact, the concept of sacrifice has existed since the beginning of time when Cain and Able both made sacrifices to God. That story also taught us something else. Some sacrifices are pleasing to God, others are not. Usually it's not the sacrifice itself that isn't pleasing, but the person's heart while making the sacrifice. The bible tells us that God likes a cheerful giver (2 Corinthians 9:7), meaning, you are sacrificing because you want to, not because you feel obligated. When you find that you are willing to sacrifice and give more freely to grow spiritually, you will also notice God giving you more, including insight to your purpose. Christ said, he who loses his life, will gain it (Mark 8:35)

Here's a good one, how about taking the time to actually **SEEK out your purpose.** We talked about patience, but that's not to be mistaken for lack of initiative. The bible can't be any clearer when it says, ask and it shall be given, seek and ye shall find, knock and the door shall be opened (Luke 11:9). Notice that each one of those contains an action that you must perform first? Asking, seeking, knocking. You must constantly ask God for direction and discernment to discover your purpose. This means prayer. Prayer is your time alone with God. A time to connect spiritually. God wants to interact with us regularly, and prayer is how we accomplish that. Just talk to him. You don't need to be elegant or a preacher. Simply close your eyes and say the things on your heart, whether they are good or bad. Many great people in the bible express their fears and doubts to God. They realized speaking to Him about it is how you overcome it. And don't be scared of a little **Pray.D.H.D** every now ant then.

Pray.D.H.D - when you convince yourself to pray, and within minutes your thoughts are distracted and more random than scrolling through a Twitter news feed. 10 minutes later you remember that you were supposed to be praying.

You must also **GET ACTIVE**. Spending too much time playing video games, watching TV, and chatting with friends on social media aren't necessarily helping you discover your purpose. Even though they aren't sins, if things are distracting you from seeking out your purpose, then your commitment and willingness to sacrifice are going to be called into question, which of course delays the process. It's simple. Get out and do the things that God is placing on your heart. You may make some mistakes. You may not always understand why. But when you are in the spirit and hearing God clearly, you can trust that He is rewarding your seeking, by brining you another step closer. Sometimes God's spirit will speak to you in a way that others may not understand right then and there. Don't worry. Your faith is your own and God has things that are only intended for you.

#ConnectW/God

When seeking out your purpose, one of the essential ingredients - **COURAGE!** Don't worry about what you have and don't have, especially when it comes to money. Don't stress over whether you are trained or not. Don't panic if there seem to be others more qualified. <u>When you read the bible, you constantly see God working through those who others least expected</u>. David was the youngest of all his brothers, had never seen battle, and yet, it would be him who killed the giant war veteran, Goliath, with nothing more than a slingshot. David didn't worry about his experience or what weapons he didn't have. He had courage and let God lead him on the path to his purpose. Look at Jesus. He wasn't born to wealthy parents. In fact, Nazareth was one of the worse areas in the region. He didn't grow up a religious scholar, and definitely wasn't some huge warrior like everyone expected of the messiah. But He had courage to rely on God to give him everything He needed to accomplish His purpose, and God never failed Him. In fact, that's why we're even able to discuss Him today. Believe that God will do the same for you. If your purpose requires you to have a degree, God will help you get through college. If your purpose means you need certain training, believe that God will help you obtain it in time. If money is a necessity, God will make sure you have exactly what you need. Trust that God will provide.

Lastly, when it comes to your purpose, never never never forget, **HAVE FUN.** God isn't some mean boss that is all work and no play. He doesn't want you stressing yourself out, because that just means you'll be a stress to others. He wants you to enjoy your life. In fact, Christ said, "I came that you may have life, and have it more abundantly (John 10:10)." It is a privilege and an honor to find and live your purpose, so if you are feeling over burdened and bummed, you may be doing something wrong. You may be focusing too much on what the bible says you can't do, instead of the infinite things you can? Maybe you're putting too much pressure on yourself to succeed? Maybe you've made some sinful mistakes or are struggling with doubt? No matter the reason, you have to trust that God knew you and your faults before you were even born, so your purpose isn't going to change for any reason. **Focus on the work and let Him handle the results.** You also may discover your purpose isn't limited to right here and now. As you learn and mature in God's word, you will see that He doesn't drop everything on you at one time. He gives you a little here and a little there, so you won't be overloaded. So your purpose this year, may evolve and grow into something bigger next year as you demonstrate your competence and success.

Believe it or not, one of the most difficult challenges you will have while pursuing your purpose won't always come from the outside world, but other Christians! Unfortunately not everybody that professes to be a Christian or goes to church will actively help you to get ahead. Even though we should all be working together to push each other since it is God's will, not our own, that we are striving for, some people have their own agenda. They can be gossipy, spiteful, cliquish, hateful and even destructive. Often times when the enemy can't get directly to us, he'll use someone that can get close to throw us off our game. Remember Judas? Just remember, things others do doesn't affect your relationship with Christ unless you let it! No matter what people may say or do, no matter what position or title they hold, nothing can stop you from accomplishing what God created you for! So don't let haters and critics have the final

<u>say, or *any* say at all for that matter.</u> Your relationship with God won't be theirs, but neither will your blessings!

Deuteronomy 11:13, 14 - ...love the LORD your God and to serve Him with all your heart and all your soul, that He will give the rain for your land in its season, the early and late rain, that you may gather in your grain and your new wine and your oil.

 I think the most important thing to remember after being saved, is that no matter how much you mature spiritually, we are always still learning and growing. Learning to read our bible and pray more diligently. Learning to let go of our guilt and pride and instead rest in God's peace. Learning to be better representatives of Christianity and how to effectively share our testimonies and speak to those who aren't saved. Learning who we can fellowship and praise God with as we seek to be around others who share similar values. Learning how fasting can help us get out of ruts and see better progress. Learning how awesome God's love and grace really is. Learning to walk in purpose. These are all areas to which there are no limits. Each will go as far as your faith allows. So continue on your path. You may have concerns about offending people or how much you should talk about your faith. There may be some friends who don't support your decision to be a Christian. Know that God never said it would be easy, but it will be worth it. Before you know it, you will be serving God through your purpose, and experiencing unimaginable blessings along the way! So here's to being saved!

NOTES:

COMFORTABLE

Not too hot, not too cold.

There is no question that being a Christian has more than its fair share of challenges. <u>Day by day, sometimes even second by second, temptations, tests of faith, sin, guilt, and distractions are waiting to capture our focus and take our minds off of God and the purpose and blessings He has for us.</u> Then you add work, school, family and friends, it can be easy to want to take a break and just relax with some free time. Not have to think. Not have to do. Just be comfortable. I think if we were to do a survey of Christians, and they were completely honest (meaning, not trying to make themselves into super religious superheroes who wear Jesus capes and fly around converting atheists), the comfortable category would probably have the highest percentage of members. On the surface, that's not a terrible thing. Being comfortable usually means at ease. Not stressing. Think – familiar. And familiar is a good thing when you consider Christian traits like salvation, relationship with God, bible study, going to church and sharing your faith. Familiar is exactly what you want to be with those things. Being comfortable is also a necessity when we think how many people talk and act negatively towards Christians. It is important to be secure in our faith when those around us have different opinions about Christ. *So why does it feel like there is a 'but' coming at any second?* You're too wise young Jedi. The problem is, comfort in this case usually means complacent, and complacency is usually the enemy of growth and satisfaction, the graveyard for progress.

In the book of Revelation (chapter 3) Jesus talks about being, "hot or cold, but not lukewarm." Meaning, you're either on fire for God, or you're not engaged at all. It's better to be struggling with sin than completely numb to it. Sitting lukewarm is really a parallel to comfortable. While there are many areas of life where being comfortable does have its advantages, our spiritual life isn't on of them. Why? It's beyond simple – **God wants us to reach our full potential and live and abundant life**. Just like family wants us to grow into successful adults (when they aren't occupied still thinking of us as their li'l babies), just like teachers want us to grow into successful students (at least that's what they claim all the homework and tests are for), God wants us to grow into successful Christians. But growing in God is not without challenges.

1) We live in a world full of material, emotional and physical distractions. Things that appear to be more tangible and immediately gratifying like money, TV shows, gadgets, social media, clothes, cars, and relationships, can often steal our time and focus.

2) The devil is a master craftsman at laying a foundation of temptation and building guilt around our sins to lock us in.

3) We aren't as knowledgeable about God and His ways as we should be.

These may not be the only ones, but they are 3 major reasons that people get trapped in the comfort zone and prevented from growing into a blessed servant like God wants. It seems like forever, now, but during the 1980s there was a popular TV show called, Lifestyles of the Rich and Famous. The host, Robin Leach, explored the extravagant homes and luxurious possessions of some of the wealthiest people on earth. Not too long after, MTV Cribs opened the doors for the public to see inside the mansions and playgrounds of celebrities. This created an interesting divide. First, you had people who didn't have those types of bank accounts, drooling and dreaming to one day live on that level of opulence. On the flip side, people who were already multimillionaires, were inspired and aspired to, 'one up,' their upper tax bracket peers. But either way, everybody began focusing their attention on one thing…money!

In fairness, riches and wealth weren't created by rock stars, oil tycoons, athletes, and software programmers. Even TV shows can't be blamed. Sure, they may have help add some popularity and jealousy, but the bible was talking about the snares of riches long before the TV was invented. Actually, I guess the bible pretty much talks about all things before they were invented. Anyway, Psalms and Proverbs, have several scriptures about the dangers of putting money ahead of God. The New Testament also touches on it several times. Here are just a few:

Proverbs 13:11: Wealth from get-rich-quick schemes quickly disappears; wealth from hard work grows over time.

Mark 8:36 For what does it profit a man to gain the whole world, and forfeit his soul?

1 Timothy 6:10: For the love of money is the root of all kinds of evil. And some people, craving money, have wandered from the true faith and pierced themselves with many sorrows

But there is probably no better example than the lure of money than Jesus and the rich young man. Matthew 19: 16-22 tells a story of a rich, young man who came to Jesus asking about eternal life. Jesus gives him 6 commandments to which the man replies he has kept them since he was young. So Jesus tells him to go sell all of his possessions and give the proceeds to the poor, then follow Jesus. The bible tells us that sadly, the man turns and leaves for he had, "great possessions."

It's intriguing to think that you could be standing right next to Jesus Christ, in the flesh and blood, the same Jesus who had probably just performed some type of never before seen miracle less than 5 minutes prior. The growing legend all over the land, Jesus, the Messiah, Jesus! Yeah, you're within arms reach, looking into His eyes, He's addressing you directly in front of the hundreds of people around, and you just turn and walk away because your cell phone and car are more important. Yet, that's what the rich young man did, because he chose his wealth over eternal life. How many of us are saying, "What an idiot! I would have never been so foolish! I would have sold everything right then and there and chased after Jesus!" Wait, let me rephrase that question, how many of us can say we would have sold everything, and been completely happy with no regrets?

For the record, Jesus fully acknowledges that we need to eat, have clothes to wear, you know, not run around naked and hungry. And He never said that having nice things is wrong or a sin. But what He does make clear, is that worrying about these things, or putting them before our relationship with God is a recipe for spiritual disaster. Why? Because anything we put before God essentially becomes an idol, and the bible is specific that we shall not have any other gods or idols before God (Exodus 20:3). We may laugh at the idea of the Israelites literally worshipping a statue of a golden calf, but is it really too much different when we think about how much money we sit around wishing we had instead of thinking about serving God? We may say we love God and all he does, but how true can that be if we don't spend a fraction of the time trying to please Him as we do trying to please/impress other people (family, friends, significant other, ourselves)? This is one of the biggest anchors for Comfortable Christians.

For most Comfortable Christians, the world is the priority. It's not intentional or planned out. It's just, well, the world we live in, literally. We can touch, smell, taste, hear and see the world around us. There are emotional connections, social pressure and the always enticing…commercials! *Buy this, not that. Wear this because that's out of season. You're not cool if you don't have the latest* _____! Sure, many Comfortable Christians go to church, pray, even read the bible, but usually those things are either a) not the highest priority or very inconsistent b) done to gain or achieve something personal c) part of the routine or status symbol. See, a lot of Comfortable Christians are knowledgeable of God and His power, but because they are more focused on worldly concerns, their relationship with God is more about what He can do for them and less about how they can serve Him. They are caught up in what they need to have, and not the sacrifices it takes to be a better Christian. As we said, there's nothing wrong when God blesses us with good things, but do they consume us? The bible (Mark 4:19) talks about how the cares of this world can be like weeds that grow up and choke the good crops, making the harvest void.

#GodWantsToBlessU!

The ironic thing, people are so worried about having stuff to stand out or relationships to feel loved, they don't realize all those things (multiplied by infinity) are what we get with God. God wants us to know real love, which is what we get with Him, not the temporary or conditional love that people give. He wants us to have the best of the best. That's why the bible (Matthew 6:33) says, seek ye first the kingdom of God and all these things will be added unto you. As Christians, we are all God's children. Just like a good parent, God rewards us when we do good, but good for God is different than what we think. He needs us to separate our thoughts and actions from the world, so the world doesn't see us as just another person chasing after gold, fame, and love. Are we paying tithes and giving offerings like we are supposed to with the resources we have? Some Christians don't pay tithes because they claim they will start once God gives them a lot of money. But money only makes you more of what you already are, so if you're not giving now, the chances that you would focus on giving when you are rich are probably still slim. That's why the world needs to see that we are Christians now, that way there is no question that all of our riches and blessings came from God himself and not just luck or hustle. When others see us blessed beyond the rest of the world, with a higher level of peace, it brings glory to God. And it may cause some others to want to follow Him too! So don't let worldly thoughts of why others have what they have or why they appear to be successful consume you. To be jealous of others is to doubt and disbelieve that God still has more in store for you.

Another reason Christians fall into the comfortable zone has to do with a battle that has been waged well before we even knew what money was to put in our first piggy bank, again, well before money and piggy banks even existed. Most of us are familiar with the story of Lucifer, the beautiful angel, being kicked out of heaven and essentially declaring war on all of God's people before he is sentenced to hell. What was the war he declared? It is an all out effort to disrupt as many Christian lives as possible. Whether keeping them from being saved or keeping them from reaching their purpose and potential, the enemy is hell bent (literally and figuratively) on ruining lives and God's kingdom.

It's actually funny when you think about it. The devil has already lost once. God already knows it's going to happen again. Yet, the enemy still scrambles around to "kill, steal, and destroy" every second of every day (John 10:10). What's not so funny, is that he is relentless and merciless in his approach. He doesn't just want to keep you away from God or God's purpose, he wants you as down and out and close to hopeless as possible. Hopelessness is like living with one foot in the grave, and that's exactly where the enemy wants you...in the grave! He knows that if you move in your God given purpose, you will be helping to change lives and restore the hope that he is working so diligently to kill. He knows you will help others get saved or move up the ladder toward servitude to God, and once they discover their purpose, God's army will continue to grow beyond measure and make this world something really special! So he is trying to stop you before you can help yourself and others. We all know it's a spiritual fight. But, many times we underestimate just how much longer the devil has been playing this game, and we get trapped because we forget the number one rule. Call on Jesus.

Have you ever stopped and looked at nature? For some of us that may be an everyday thing. For others who live in a more metropolitan area, it might not be a regular occurrence. But no matter how often you see it, there is no denying God's majesty when we can look at a nice natural setting, even if it's just a screen saver! Now take that beauty and multiply it by infinity, because that's what the Garden of Eden had to have looked like. God's paradise untouched by man's hands until Adam and Eve came along, and we all know what happened shortly after that.

#Evicted!

The truth is, many of us would have fallen victim to the same traps the serpent left for Eve and Adam. How do I know? Because it was the same banana peel tactic that most of us still slip on from time to time now - **temptation.** At this point I think it's fair to say temptation is literally the enemy's oldest trick in the book. It worked then. It works now. Why change a good thing. But another less focused on ploy he used in that same passage and continues to use on us – **guilt**. See, first he tempted Eve to sin by eating the forbidden fruit. Then he immediately made her feel guilty for what she did so she ran to Adam and tempted him to eat some too, so she wouldn't be the only who had done wrong. Once Adam's guilt kicked in, he tried hiding from God, and just like a man - blaming Eve! "That woman you created made me do it (Genesis 3:12)!" LOL. Nothing like manning up and taking ownership. But for any of us, when we aren't careful, temptation can lead to sin, sin leads to guilt, and guilt leads to a disconnect from God. And that disconnect pushes us further away from things we should be doing like seeking God's will and pursuing our purpose. Too chained in guilt to make a move.

When we allow the guilt to hinder us too frequently or over too long a period of time, it often leads to pessimism and doubt that cause us to be trapped in the comfortable Christian zone. #BreakYourBox!

We know that sin is a result of our own action. Fortunately, we know that each and every one of our sins, no matter how big or small has been forgiven. So how is the enemy still able to use guilt to trip us up so badly? When we dissect it, the roots really begin with the temptation. In case you didn't know, temptation is not our fault. It is the devil trying to entice us or lure us into something we shouldn't be a part of. Whether it is as simple as little white lie or as extreme as breaking the law, the enemy will always try to get us to do something that violates what God wants us to do. It's nothing new. We mentioned Adam and Eve, but he has also tempted every person in the bible since them, including Jesus. We know temptation is going to happen, the bible tells us we will be tested (James 1:2-4). I'm being tempted not to keep writing this book and go do something else, as I'm writing. You're probably being tempted to do something other than read this book. Make no mistake, the enemy will try any and everything to get us from doing what will help us grow in God! BUT, the bible also tells us that we will never face any temptation greater than what we can handle (1 Corinthians 10:13). That's part of the reason why the guilt eats us up.

The uncut truth is that temptation is simply a choice. A choice to do one thing or another. In the spiritual case, it is a choice to follow the voice of God, or follow that of the enemy.

Just like how the angel and devil sit on cartoon character's shoulders and each whispers good or bad suggestions. Except in the case of temptation, only God whispers the right thing to do. The devil yells, screams, blatantly throws it in your face, works hard to get you to do wrong. He doesn't respect free will as much as God. BUT, despite whatever method he uses to tempt us, it's still our choice to do or not to do. And that's part of the reason why the guilt can seem so heavy after we sin. It feels as if we let God down. As if we chose the enemy over God. In some cases it may seem like we won't ever have what it takes to follow God perfectly like He deserves, so why even bother. Some even tell themselves, *"I may as well not even focus on God since I won't be able to live up to the standard"*. In fact, there is a Christian term, "backsliding," that suggests we have given up doing the right things in Christ and instead go through a period of sliding back into worldly ways. But the truth is, once we're saved, we are saved. There is nothing short of renouncing God that can add or take away from that salvation. Sure, God is much more pleased when we dedicate our saved lives to serving Him, but to me "backsliding," suggests we actually achieved something and then went backwards again. When the bible is clear, **everything we are and have is by God's grace.** We don't earn any of it, lest any man should boast (Ephesians 2:8-9). Instead of "backsliding," I think a better way to think of it would be, disconnected. Making the mistake of putting sin or worldly desires ahead of our commitment to God. We'll call it, **Hide 'n' Go Creep.**

Hide 'n Go Creep - When you're doing things you know you shouldn't be doing, so you stay away from praying and God as if he can't see you.

But whether this has happened once or one million times, we can't completely overlook the most important factor…Christ's blood!

When the devil is most successful at disrupting Christian lives, is when he can convince people that they aren't worthy of God's love, and 10 times out of 10 that has to do with magnifying their guilt and minimizing Christ's sacrifice. Our sins are just a mistake. That's it. No matter if it is the same sin 100 times, or 100 new sins one time each, they are all just mistakes, and God knows it! The Apostle Paul talks about, "doing what I hate and not doing what I love (Romans 7: 15-20)," because it was important that we understand our mistakes/sins are inevitable. Rather than beating ourselves up, trust in Christ's forgiveness and keep moving forward, passed the mistakes and passed the guilt. *"Yeah, but you don't know how many times I have sinned, Rickey. You don't know how bad my sins are."* IT DOESN'T MATTER! IT DOESN'T MATTER! IT DOESN'T MATTER! *Does it matter?* IT DOESN'T MATTER! That is why the bible dedicates so many scriptures to forgiveness and God's grace. God wants us to be sure that He knows all of our sins and imperfections and He chooses to love and bless us anyway so we can stay connected to Him. That's what makes Him so amazing!

Guilt is nothing more than the enemy pulling the strings of our pride. That our mistakes are somehow greater than what our all-knowing, been around since the beginning of time, aware of everything that will ever happen, messiah, Jesus's blood accounted for. #BloodOfLife

---

1 John 1:9 - If we confess our sins, he is faithful and just and will forgive us our sins and purify us from all unrighteousness.

Psalms 103:12 - He has removed our sins as far from us as the east is from the west.

Ephesians 1:7 - In him we have redemption through his blood, the forgiveness of sins, in accordance with the riches of God's grace

2 Corinthians 12:9 - ...My grace is sufficient for you, for my power is made perfect in weakness."

So the next time you feel temptation coming on, step away and pray. Call on Jesus. Pray hard. <u>Push past the **Pray.D.H.D** and pray like you're in a fight for your life, because in a sense you are.</u> But even during those times when you don't have the strength to resist, don't let your pride get in the way. Ask God for forgiveness, trust that it has been given, and get back to doing God's work. God factored all your mistakes into your purpose and blessings. If the temptation or sin seems to overbearing, speak to a friend, pastor, or counselor. There is nothing wrong with getting help from a trustworthy or professional source to help overcome problems. In fact, if more people weren't so worried about the stigma of speaking about their problems to trained professionals, we would have more people actually okay, instead of pretending to be okay. **God gives some people special knowledge and insight to help others.** It is their purpose. Many times they had to overcome their own sin and guilt to reach the level they have, so they are able to help from personal experience, not just God's word.

Which brings us to the 3rd reason why many Christians get stuck in the comfortable zone - they aren't familiar with God and all His mysterious ways. Sounds like a bit of an oxymoron. How can we be *familiar* with *mysterious* ways? Really we can't. We may never know why God does the things He does, or allows things to happen, but we can be familiar with His nature, and that's really all we need. God's nature is one of love that we can't even comprehend. If we knew how much good He wanted for us, we wouldn't need to chase after money, people, or material things, because He would give us exactly what would make us happiest. Have you ever had your mind set on something, but somebody gave you something else? At first you were skeptical, but then found out it was even better than what you wanted? That's God to the infinite degree. He wants to give us the very best, including the desires of our heart and a clear conscience. So if we knew how merciful God was, we would never feel guilt from our mistakes because we would understand that His forgiveness is the equivalent of the mistake never happening. You know those times you wish you could rewind time and get a "do-over?" That's exactly what God gives us! Only we don't need to rewind time, the sins and mistakes were already erased when Jesus covered them with his blood.

God wants more for us than we want for ourselves! #GetYourBlessings!

Unlike us, He doesn't have the distractions of the flesh to cloud what's really good and what isn't. And of course He has that, omniscient, omnipotent, time eternal, creator of the universe advantage too. But we will never even scratch the surface of His ways (or love for us) if we don't get out of the comfort zones and explore! Don't have a church home? Get out there and explore churches until the spirit of God tells you where to be. Don't read your bible or pray regularly? Don't cheat and just memorize a few scriptures to quote in order to show off. Force yourself to break the chains of complacency and make time right now. Set a schedule if you have to. Don't just do things for social status like so many other comfortable Christians. Explore ministries at your church where you may be able to volunteer. Explore fellowship circles that are going to challenge you! Many times we get intimidated by people who know more about the bible or who appear to be, "more Christian," than us. But those are the people you want to hang around. Not only can they help pull you out of your comfort zone, you will quickly discover they make mistakes and are trying to grow too! The more you get involved with God, the more you will learn how great He is and how much greatness He has for you! People spend thousands of dollars going to psychics for a false glimpse into the future, millions of dollars playing the lottery for an improbable chance at wealth, and countless hours chasing love, when God has all those things waiting for us, if we only learn His ways.

The reality is, we are all in a war. I'm not talking about a war overseas, or a war on the latest political hot button. No, this is a war on souls. If someone walked up and pushed us for no reason, not many of us would pull our cell phones out and start tweeting what we were having for dinner. If they pushed us again, I'm sure we wouldn't go to YouTube and start watching clips of cats doing funny things. We'd be irritated, upset, questioning what was going on. Many would be ready to fight back! Yet, in spiritual attacks we often sit comfortably because we can't physically see or feel what is happening, but it is happening behind the scenes. The bible (Ephesians 6:12) says we wrestle not against the flesh and blood, but powers and principalities that can't be seen. Those powers and principalities are after your happiness, your salvation and your life! And in any battle when a soldier is guarding his life, he puts on the proper armor. We need to be putting on the full armor of God from the time we wake up, to our final prayer of the day before going to bed, because the enemy never stops waging war.

What is that proper armor? Because it's a spiritual war it's only right that we have spiritual equipment. Ephesians 6:10-18 tells of the God issued weaponry we will need to fight for our purpose and prosperity. The belt of truth, breastplate of righteousness, shoes of peace, shield of faith, helmet of salvation, and sword of the spirit (which is the word of God). I know, some of you gamers are saying, that doesn't sound half as exciting as the gear in Call of Duty! True, there are no cinematic explosions or long range weaponry. Come to think about it, there aren't even bows and arrows! But I'm guessing there is a reason for that, and that reason is because this spiritual battle is one that happens closer than we can imagine, so up close personal protection is a must!

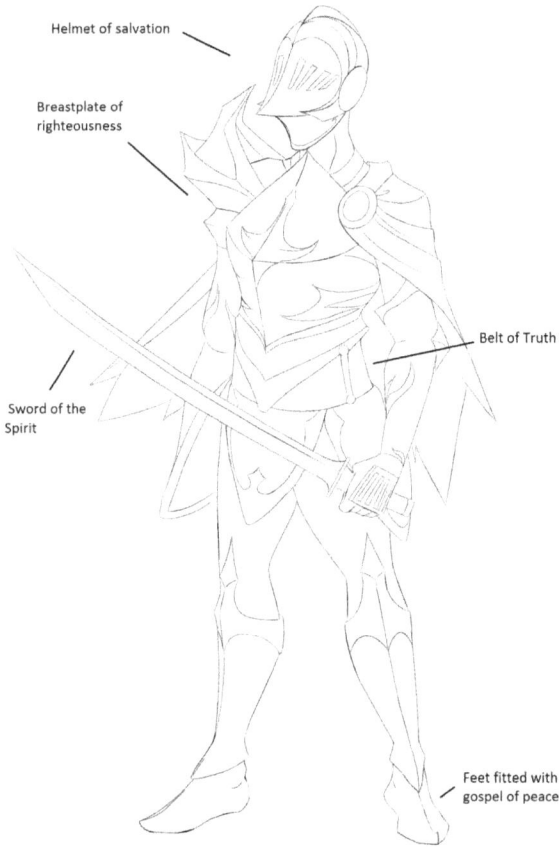

As you can see, all the vital areas are protected, and this is based on technology from more than 2,000 years ago.

Still, sometimes comfort is just a byproduct of too much doubt setting in and losing sight of God's awesome and miracle working power. You may have suffered a few setbacks that you didn't quite understand, been disappointed a time or two in requests not being granted, and before you know it your faith has waivered off. <u>You never stopped believing that God exists, but your actions and words don't reflect that He is capable of doing what He says.</u> Comfortable is a classic example of faith coming up short. I'm not saying that in a derogatory way, just want folks to understand that if faith is the substance of things hoped for (Hebrews 11:1), once you remove the hopeful expectation of God being able to do wonderful things, your faith sinks too. We forget that God knows all, and sometimes His answer to what we want is, "no," or, "not yet," because He knows it won't be good for us or we're just not ready. So we lose faith when we don't get our way and less faith means less favor, until eventually you just sit comfortable not expecting anything miraculous. God would love to bless us with more, because He knows the more He blesses us, the more glory He gets from people seeing His presence in our lives. **Everyone, even the best preachers, have times when their faith gets shaky.** The difference is that rather than getting comfortable in their hope or actions, they work even harder (like a servant) to find out what God wants, instead of focusing on what they wanted but didn't get. Understand, faith doesn't come easy for anybody, but it will never come at all if you don't exercise it. Faith is like a muscle. Work it out until you reach, **Miracle Faith!**

Miracle Faith – <u>not minimizing what God can do. Expecting miracles despite all the doubt from others around you. Not being afraid to speak on and work towards the unexplainable things God can do.</u>

The comfortable category isn't one that's looked at as some bible thumping, holier than thou, wannabe saint. Which is good! This is a category where people can have a regular conversation without trying to figure out a way to tie Christ into it, or go around making others uncomfortable or defensive about their own personal beliefs. Which is something that God appreciates. But on the flip side, <u>He doesn't want any of us soooo comfy that others can't even tell we are Christians.</u> What He really wants is balance. It's not the sin, guilt, material desires, understanding, etc., it's really the time management! No Christian has or will be perfect, but the truly successful ones recognized that we have a limited time on this earth, and the best way to make the most of it is to serve God, because not only does He deserve it, but ultimately He can do more for us than we can ever do for ourselves. God wouldn't complain if we spent every waking hour worshipping Him and spreading His word, but He also understands better than anyone (He is the one that created us after all) that we are human, and we have families, friends, hobbies, school, work, etc. that we will inevitably end up devoting time to as well. He just asks for our first fruits, and that's not just referring to money. Time, heart, soul, commitment - service!

Remember: Hot or Cold! #NoLukewarm!

Understand, bad traits don't make you a bad person. No need to be defensive, just stop and pray. Those times when you're bored or looking for something on TV, recognize the opportunity to connect with God. Don't look to fill your time with worldly things. Christianity should never be comfortable. The enemy is always waging war that we need to be prepared for and there's always a new level we can grow to. Don't compromise your purpose and blessings for comfort! Purpose helps push beyond the insignificant and distractions. It is a motivator and an energizer. When we wake up in the morning we should be reading a few scriptures from the bible to get our mind spiritually awakened.

Having the word on your heart before you do anything else will influence what you say and do all throughout the day. And the more you spend your day doing for His benefit, the more He will do for yours. So get out of your comfort zone and move into servitude. Christianity isn't about self preservation or guilt release, God wants us serving Him. It may mean more work, but that's why you never hear success stories from the lazy! Remember, being saved is for our benefit. Serving and strengthening God's kingdom is how we give back to Him!

NOTES:

SERVANT
On the job for God

High five! When it comes to Christianity, this is where God wants us all to be. I know, I know, being a servant doesn't sound like the most flattering title. Generally when we think of servants, we think of people with worn out and beat up clothes who are forced to take orders, don't have any rights or say over their life, maybe not good enough to do for themselves. But that is not the case when it comes to Christianity. We know that God gave us free will, so 1) being a servant to God is a conscious decision you have made, not something you had to do. 2) If you truly believe God is the creator and ruler of everything, then serving Him should really be viewed as an honor and privilege. 3) If we really love Him even a fraction of how much He loves us, then we prove it by serving Him! The plans that God has for us are good, so He makes available whatever we need to serve Him and fulfill our purpose, because the only way we can serve is in our purpose.

Many confuse being saved as the grand finale of our spiritual journey, but it is actually just the beginning. The goal is not being saved. Salvation is just for you. The goal is purpose, which doesn't happen until the servant level because of the deeper understanding and commitment you have once you reach here. Your heart is in it. You understand that God deserves our all and are willing to give your all to fulfilling your purpose.

<u>There are 4 main objectives to spiritual purpose.</u>

1) Glorify God
2) Save and strengthen God's kingdom
3) Demonstrate God's unconditional love
4) Get your true blessings!

Some may contest that you don't have to know your purpose to be a servant of God, but we don't even have to pull scriptures to justify this one. **What servant can actually, serve, if they aren't given at least a vague idea of what they are supposed to be accomplishing?** *Well, as long as we are talking about God and helping others get saved, we are serving God.* I disagree. That sounds logical, but if we were to pull scripture, like say, Matthew 7:22,23, it addresses that claim the best. "Many will say to me on that day, 'Lord, Lord, did we not prophesy in your name, and in your name drive out demons and perform many miracles? Then I will tell them plainly, 'I never knew you. Away from me, you evildoers!" <u>Jesus makes it very clear that just because we do things for Him or in His name, doesn't mean we are serving Him</u>. Think about it, we know that any sustainable kingdom must have numerous servants that are all skilled in certain areas. Otherwise it will fall apart. If you had a baseball team with all pitchers, who would play first base, catcher, etc.? In order to be effective, you need everybody to be the best at their position, not trying to play the role of others. Just like Paul said (1 Corinthians 12:12-27), the body has many different parts, and none is more important than the other because all of them work together for one purpose! That is why you are only truly a servant of God when you are living your purpose in the body of Christ.

Your purpose will be a passion that help change lives, which means you are changing the world. #Destiny

It may sound pessimistic, but I honestly don't think most Christians ever fulfill their purpose. Many flat out never discover it. Others may know theirs, but don't have the courage and commitment to believe or act on it, and still others may know and try, but just not follow through in the ways God specifically wants. So being a servant actually puts you in very distinguished company. And it's not that other Christians don't want to serve, but it takes a lot of sacrifice and commitment to bond with God and learn what He has designed for you. Life can throw out a lot of temptations and distractions, and not everybody will successfully and consistently overcome them, so they are prevented from reaching their full spiritual potential. It doesn't make them less of a Christian, because saved is saved. It doesn't mean God loves them any less, because He loves us all equally. It just means that they didn't or won't achieve on the level and receive the blessings they could have. And one of, if not the main reason for that…FAITH!

Faith is critical. It is faith that helps servants maneuver through those same distractions and temptations that hang up others. Faith makes us realize how much time and attention God deserves. Faith strengthens us in times of weakness. Faith gives us a vision of how much we can accomplish if we trust in the Lord. Faith cancels out fear, and pushes us to take action rather than sit around worrying. There are so many negatives in life, from anchoring guilt to memorable disappointments that hinder people's faith. But not servants. To achieve this level, you have demonstrated a tremendous level of faith, and God has obviously rewarded you for it in order to keep you moving closer to Him. In fact, your faith and the work you did in faith were both clearly pleasing enough to God, that he revealed (or is revealing) His purpose for you.

Faith allows us to see what many cannot, because it may not be visible in the physical realm. #SpiritualLenses

It will take a lot of faith to see your purpose, whatever it may be, all the way through. The harder you work, the more the devil will attack. Remember, the more you are fulfilling your purpose in God's kingdom, the more you are tearing the enemy's down. He came to kill, steal, and destroy, but your purpose in God helps to save and strengthen, that's as opposite as opposite can get! So of course the devil wants to disrupt you. **But like everything in life, to grow you must be tested, and to be tested, means being challenged beyond what you're used to.** High school classes don't test you on Middle School material. College doesn't give mid-terms on elementary school lessons. You will be tested on what you are learning then and there, so it will be tougher than what you went through in the past. But have faith! The bible tells us that not only will God be with us (Psalm 147:3), but that we are capable of all things if we keep our faith in Christ to bring us through (Philippians 4:13). God not only wants you to achieve your purpose, He wants you to enjoy it, so He blesses you for it so that others can see how great He works in His servants, and they may be inspired to serve too. Everybody wins! Well, everybody but the devil, of course. He's only happy when we are sick with **Spiritual Bulimia.**

<u>Spiritual Bulimia – praying and then worrying, which completely pushes out your faith.</u>

It also takes faith to willingly and constantly make changes of dropping habits and characteristics that aren't pleasing to God or that contradict the lessons in the bible. Being a servant means you represent your master's values, and this isn't always easy, wait, it's almost never easy when we are talking about the standards Christ set. Biting your tongue when you really want to yell at someone, showing patience to those who work your nerves, setting a positive standard that others respect, forgiving people even though they didn't apologize, and these are just a few everyday examples of what you will deal with. In a world where so many people put themselves first and usually don't take others into consideration, embodying the many principles that the Word of God teaches will be tough, make no mistake. But the great thing is that Christ went through those same issues during His time on earth. He knows some people will deliberately try to upset you. Others won't do it intentionally, but that doesn't make it any less annoying. <u>Christ knows we may slip up every now and then, but it is our faith that God loves us unconditionally that allows us to seek forgiveness and try again (Proverbs 24:16).</u> In fact, we keep trying until the day we have gone on to be with the Lord. So don't be scared to be honest with God when you get irritated or frustrated, or any other feelings. Talk to Him. May as well get it off your chest, because it's not like He doesn't know already. LOL. But one way we can make this whole process simpler, focus on humility. We live in an age where reality TV shows and social media has everyone feeling like they are celebrities. 5,000 plus friends and I'm pretty positive 4,995 of them could care less about an average Wednesday dinner, but someone still felt the need to post the pics. Thousands of followers just to say, "I have thousands of followers," because really there is no communication or common ground. Reality shows about people with no apparent talent gone well beyond their 15 minutes of fame. You get the point, many people feeling like their life deserves the limelight. I'm not here to dispute who is important and who isn't, just to remind you of one of the most essential characteristics of a servant – humility.

When we truly understand God's love and mercy, we realize it is all about Him and there is no room for egos. #PrideAside

Humility is what reminds us that we are here to serve God and not our own appetites or ego. Humility is what keeps our pride at bay. It is a necessity because the devil uses pride as a gateway to foster arrogance, and arrogance will commonly lead to a sense of entitlement, selfishness, and lack of patience, which coincidentally, are all on the opposite end of the servitude spectrum! The bible speaks at length on pride versus humility for a reason. There were many who fell out of God's will because of their pride. You could actually start with Lucifer, who according to the book of Revelation thought he was better than God and got banished from heaven where he would become Satan, or the devil, and sentenced to eternal damnation. There are two very interesting, and often misperceived points to that story. 1) God never even had to fight Lucifer. How inflated was the devil's ego if he thought he was better than God, but couldn't even beat God's number 2 guy? Imagine what God would have done if He did step in himself. Scary. 2) Satan was not given the title as ruler or master of hell, like many movies or stories proclaim. Satan will be in as much misery, if not more, than everybody else, which is why he is working so hard to drag down as many other people as he can. His pride got him kicked out of heaven, now his pride won't let him spend eternity alone.

That's just the beginning. There was Samson who was deceived into believing he was the source of his own strength, and not God. There was David who slept with one of his best friends wife and then had that friend killed. There was Paul who had Christians persecuted and killed prior to his conversion. The bible is filled with stories of pride leading people down the wrong path. <u>Fortunately, those same stories always involve God intervening and forgiving because He knows we are human</u>. God is never looking to punish us, but sometimes we must learn the lesson or deal with the consequences of our decisions. Pride is characteristic that God wants to see purged from our system because it is not a quality that helps us serve Him or show love to others. Pride typically indicates an, I am important attitude. I did that well. I deserve this. I am better. **It's no coincidence that the 'I' in, pride, is right in the middle, because pride usually suggests that, "I" deserve to be the center of attention.** This can especially be the case when you are serving God. Think about it. You are making sacrifices that others aren't. You are helping people discover and renew their life in God. You are carrying out a very important purpose. It doesn't take much for the devil to step in and try to convince you that you are better than other Christians. Or that you deserve more for all the work you do. In fact, the devil even tried the same approach with Jesus (Matthew 4:1-11).

After coming off of a 40 day fast, the devil tried to appeal to Jesus' pride with power and fame. When Jesus refused, the devil tried to contort the scripture and play off Jesus' pride, being that he was the Son of God. We obviously know that Jesus resisted, and went on to great glory, but there are many lessons that we can learn from this story to help keep your pride in check and go on to the greatness that God has waiting for you.

1) The devil will attack anybody. Some Christians feel they are immune or too strong in the spirit for the devil to bother them, but if his pride was big enough to think he could influence the Son of God, then you and I are definitely not off limits. A fish swims. A bird flies. The devil deceives. In any fight or war, one of the most basic guidelines is to never underestimate your enemy. If you let your guard down for a second, he will take advantage. God can and will protect you, but you have to remember to pray and prepare.

2) The devil won't stop attacking. Even when Jesus corrected him, he immediately tried again. Just because you beat him once, doesn't mean the fight is over. He will continue to attack you for as long you are alive. When one approach doesn't work, he will quickly try another. He will keep on trying because his pride will not allow him to believe he has already failed. This is one reason the bible tells us, pray without ceasing (1 Thessalonians 5:17). As long as we are on this earth, we will need God's protection and discernment to stay on the path of our purpose.

3) He will attack with even more energy when he thinks you are at your weakest. Jesus was in the desert for 40 days fasting. Obviously He didn't have the same strength and

energy that He normally would, so what did the devil do? He tried to slide in real cool and calm, hoping that Jesus would submit to his bribes. When you are going through difficult times, expect the devil to try and creep in. Whether it's a disagreement with friends or parents, school or financial situation, remember that the devil will not have any sympathy and will try to tempt your pride. Don't let him.

4) Lastly, the devil knew the scripture and tried to twist it for his personal gain. Remember, just because people can quote the bible does not mean they have you or God's best interest in mind. Some may sound sincere, but have very selfish ambitions or ulterior motives. That is why we rely on God. If we let our pride get in the way, we may not be able to separate the truth from the fiction or good offers from God's offers.

In Philippians 2, Paul puts the icing on the cake when it comes to humility. He talks about how even though Christ was equal to God, He still acted as if He was a servant. Think about it. Christ didn't live in a fancy mansion or ride around in an expensive chariot. He didn't wear fine linens or fragrances. For His grand entrance, He actually rode in on a donkey, not an expensive stallion. Despite the fact that people were willing to pay Him. Despite the fact He could have taken over by force if He wanted or that people tried to force Him into a position of authority, <u>Jesus humbled himself, and God gave Him the most popular, powerful name to exist in human history.</u> For you and I, there is nothing wrong with having nice things if God blesses us with them, but we must never forget that nothing we have is because of our work or who we are. It is because God is gracious and loving. The more we remember that, the more we will grow in humility and spiritual maturity.

Wheew! Seem like a lot to digest already? That's just the tip of the iceberg. Being a servant will have other challenges as well. One big one will be, isolation. Not that you have to be a loner, but **often the higher you go in any career field, the fewer people you encounter that posses your same level of drive, initiative, and work ethic.** It's the same with Christianity. Isolation doesn't mean you intentionally separate yourself from everybody else either. Remember, as a humble servant you want to extend yourself to others in fellowship. It just means that where God wants to lead you is meant for you, and you can't expect others to be on that same path. They have their own purpose to fulfill and heights to reach. Isolation doesn't mean you'll be alone all the time either. There will be times when you laugh and pray and build with others, and there will be times when you need to be by yourself. Sometimes isolation won't be physical. You can be in a crowded room and still feel alone because people don't think spiritually like you. There were times when even Jesus would get frustrated at His disciples because they weren't focused spiritually like Him (although He did have a something of a slight advantage LOL), but there were other times when He would patiently explain the point they missed. It boiled down to balance.

Like in all walks of your Christian life, like we mentioned previously in this book, balance is always a factor. Just like you need a balance of bible study, worship, and prayer, you also need a balance of isolation and fellowship. There are times when conversations with friends or brothers/sisters in Christ helps give you a new perspective on your walk. Other times, you may need to be alone for God to speak to you directly. Balance. There are many people who are going to be astonished by your spiritual maturity, and there are haters who are going to call you a know it all and hypocrite. There are those who are going to always seek your opinions, advice and prayer, and still others who you have to make an effort to reach out to. Again, what's that word? Balance. Just know that there were times when Christ had to stand alone. He realized that there is no relationship more important than a person's direct connection to God. Friends, family, classmates, co-workers, church family, I could go on and on. Always remember that no matter how many people you know and how regularly you talk with them, there are going to be times when you find yourself on your own. And that's okay! Because the truth is you are never really alone, God is always there with you. And isn't that the relationship we need to develop the most? Yeah, FaceBook, Twitter, Instagram, Skype, Snap Chat, FaceTime, text messages are great ways to stay in contact with your friends, but none of that will do you any good if you haven't strengthened the foundation that all your relationships will be built on…God! So be comfortable in all things and situations, keep an open mind to the challenges and changes that are constantly occurring, and know that even when others aren't on your level, you are never really standing alone, because God is always right there with you.

The world has known no greater love than Christ's love for us. #RealRelationship

Remember, being a servant won't ever mean you're perfect. And that's good news because now none of us ever have to worry about being perfect. We will always battle with temptation and sin because the enemy will never quit.

Unlike some may allege, being a servant doesn't mean you know everything, because we couldn't even write about God's infinite knowledge if every ocean suddenly turned into ink. Being a servant simply means you understand God blessed you with life and special abilities to help build and strengthen His kingdom, and you are doing your best to achieve that.

There will still be plenty of mistakes and shortcomings, truthfully, there may be more! Because the more you strive to learn about God's word and your purpose in it, the more accountable you will become because of the information you have. Knowledge is not only power, it is a responsibility. But even then, not everything will always go the way you think. We can expect disappointment like everyone else. And it's not because God doesn't love us or we're wrong about something, it's that sometimes we get ahead of ourselves and God's timetable. As long as we apply our mistakes to future planning to avoid making them again, we are growing. God knows where we really are and where He needs us to be, that's why He allows things to not always go our way. He understands it's the adversity that helps us grow!

In fact, many Christians are scared of the servant level for that reason alone. They don't want the responsibility or pressure of being on this level, because amongst other reasons, they are fearful they won't be able to live up to the standards set by the world, or sometimes other Christians. But that is the beauty of being on this level, **you are constantly reassured that it doesn't matter what other people say, it's all about what God says!** And God said we all fall short of his glory (Romans 3:23), meaning none of us have been or ever will be perfect like Jesus. So being a servant and disciple isn't about perfection. It's about faith, focus, work and a little bit of patience.

We often lose sight that God and our salvation are eternal, meaning there is no beginning and no end. If you were to take away our clocks and calendars how would we function? Would we still rush here and there? Would we always have our phones out to call or text this person or that person? What would life be like without time constraints? Would we be more patient if we didn't count only 24 hours in a day or 7 days in a week to get things done? One day in heaven we may have a better understanding of eternal, but in the meantime it's important you use what you know to practice patience. Patience with yourself that mistakes are inevitable and growth is a process. Patience with others so that that they can see a positive representation of Christianity and understand a fraction of God's patience with us.

Patience doesn't mean you let people walk over you or treat you in a disrespectful manner. **Don't confuse patience with being gullible or too tolerant**. There were times when Jesus allowed people to express freely, and there were other times when He got straight to the point, it all depended on the situation. In your life you should keep a temperature track. Do you get upset or annoyed with others easily? Do you put unreasonable expectations on yourself? Can you pray and read the bible every day, but as soon as your parents say something you don't agree with, you go ballistic? Those are just a few signs that you have to work on your patience. But the good news is that we all need to work on our patience. Sometimes that may mean not being around certain people or environments. Other times it may mean counting to ten and saying a quick prayer to cool down before you speak. Concentrate on the obvious areas first. Recognize where you admittedly need more patience, and pray and work on it. You should see the number of outbursts or irritations consistently go down. If you normally get mad at your younger brother or sister twenty times a week, work on cutting it down to fifteen times, then ten, then five, until eventually you're completely unaffected by their behavior (even though you may think they are most annoying sibling on the planet). But no matter what your scenario or area to work on, be patient with yourself. If God is patient with you, and He's the one who called you to be a servant (and to be patient), then shouldn't you obey?

Life may be short, but patience can help us enjoy every second of it! #ToTheFullest

The best way to build your patience (and every area of your life) is prayer. We've mentioned it before, but really can't mention it enough. Prayer is your time to disconnect from the distractions and temptations of the physical world and get directly in tune with God. Despite being a servant ranking at the top of the list, it is now more than ever you have to remember to practice the basics of what got you here. Dealing with new levels of trials will take new levels of prayerful focus. Remembering to pray consistently is the best way to make sure you are staying on the path to your purpose.

When you realize you're salvation and purpose ties into a much bigger plan that God has structured, everyday life should take on a new meaning. Continue to study the bible, praise God, and pray each and every day. Fellowship and fast regularly. Always push to exercise the humility, patience, and faith that Jesus exemplified when He showed us all how to serve in a way that helps build and strengthen God's kingdom. There are always ways in which we can grow, so never stop challenging yourself. Wouldn't want to fall into the Comfortable category now would we? Lastly, never ever ever ever forget, HAVE FUN and ENJOY! **You have been called by God and that is something to be excited about! He chose you! So live your purpose with a smile on your face.** Get excited every morning about how God will work through you! Even when you aren't having the best day or things aren't making sense, trust that God's plans always come together and He will not leave you stranded! Take your, **Servant's Breath.**

Servant's breath: breathe in and imagine the entire universe. All the planets and living creations that have ever existed. Feel God's presence in and all around, not just in heaven. Recognize the life and power being given to complete your tasks. Inhale greatness. Exhale miracles. There is no gravity, just complete release in God's Spirit. Show your miracle faith!

Your enthusiasm will not only change many lives, but one day God will tell you, "well done good and faithful servant!"

NOTES:

SERVANT

FANATIC
All God, all the time

Sometimes when I think about how grand, merciful, giving, wise, holy, loving, omniscient, forgiving, whew, not sure I have enough paper to list every possible adjective that can describe God, plus I'm sure you get the point, so let's just go with- really really amazing. When my little mind tries to grasp God's greatness, it's hard not to want to be a fanatic for Him. It's not like fanatic is a bad word. Plus, God deserves so much more than what we actually give, and even at our very best we could never give all He actually deserves. Which brings us right back to how good He is, because He still loves us infinitely regardless! That alone is worth fanatical praise and devoted love.

Praise and love. Did you know those are two of the most mentioned commands in the bible? <u>Our praise is what proves our appreciation and reverence for God, and our love is what demonstrates His work in us</u>. Society shouts and applauds for entertainers and celebrities all the time. We praise material items like luxury homes and automobiles as if they fell from heaven. So one of the great things about being on the fanatic level is the recognition of how much more praise God deserves than things of this world.

We love our friends and family so we message, video chat, etc. on a regular basis. Many people often get so consumed in love with boy/girl friends they may not think about anyone else for days. We love certain restaurants and foods, fashion styles, TV shows, etc., so much that we think about them all the time. But how much love is society at large showing to God? Again, one of the great attributes of the Fanatic level is the understanding that we shouldn't love anything more than God himself.

But like everything else, God is a god of order and balance, and balance is one of the main areas of improvement on every level, fanatic is no exception. Why? Because on the Fanatic level Christians are most often perceived by others to be too caught up with our own personal beliefs and opinions to be concerned about anyone else who doesn't talk or think like us. We think we are doing right by God, but the truth is, even if we could dedicate every waking minute to praying and praising God, I'm certain that isn't what He wants. Oh, make no mistake, God loves to be praised and I'm not suggesting we shouldn't praise Him. The bible is clear on that (Psalm 92:1). But, the bible is also very clear that He could make the rocks praise Him if He really wanted (Luke 19:40). BTW- tell me you wouldn't freak out if you were walking along minding your own business when suddenly a bunch of rocks broke out in a chorus of Amazing Grace! Wait, would that be considered…Christian Rock? Wait again, did I really just go there? Unfortunately I did.

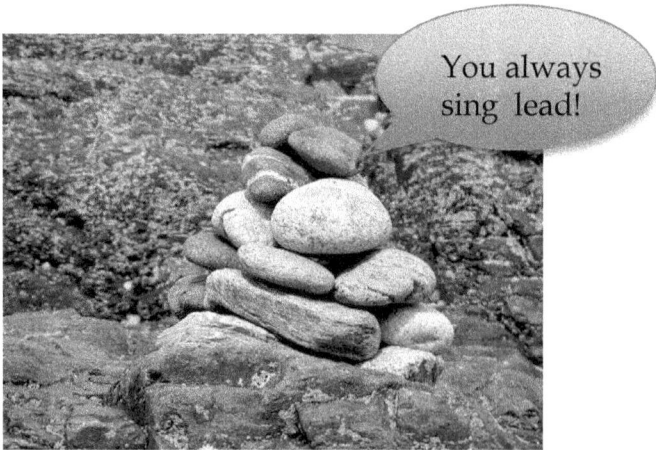

You always sing lead!

So what's the connection between praise, love, and balance? On the fanatic level it's usually this: <u>a better portion of praising and representing God needs to be done through loving actions toward others.</u> Unfortunately many people on the fanatic level miss that point, and can come across as judgmental, closed minded, unconcerned, overbearing, and even disrespectful. I don't think anyone intends to be that way, but when we look at the definition of fanatic, that's what is suggests. True story, as I was creating the labels for each chapter of this book, I kicked around several ideas for each before praying and letting God show me which to settle on. So I started typing this chapter, and about half way through realized I hadn't looked up the exact definition of fanatic. So I jumped on Google, typed in fanatic and the first three definitions that popped up (Google, Dictionary.Reference and Merriam-Webster) all used religion as part of their examples. Religion? Yep, not people pushing and shoving in a mosh pit at their favorite band's concert. Not shirtless fans in below zero weather with their faces painted yelling at sports teams. Not even shoppers who miss Thanksgiving because they want to camp outside of stores for a week just to catch the best deals. Nope, fanatic was used for people who act like their way is the only way when it comes to religious beliefs. <u>This means Christians have been lumped into the same category as zealots who use bombs and guns to intimidate others, cults who commit mass suicides, and secluded groups who don't even function in society.</u> I think you and I can agree that is not how Jesus wants to be remembered. Radical? Yes. Fanatic? Not even close.

So how do we ensure that we don't get trapped on the fanatic level, but also not compromise our faith in Jesus? How can we relate to the real world on a spiritual level? How do we speak to nonbelievers in practical terms if they don't want to hear about the bible? I think the bible gives us a few keys steps on how to praise, love, and share the truth of God, without being called the f word. And it starts with humility.

There is definitely an empowering and conquering freedom that comes with worshipping Christ. An understanding that we can do all and accomplish all because we have His power working within us. Yet, despite all the ways we recognize God for all He has done for us, in the blink of an eye we can forget it was Him and allow pride to deceive us into believing that we are somehow responsible, or that we are better, more knowledgeable, more committed than someone else. Think of the Pharisees in the bible. They were supposed to be the highest ranking servants of God, yet, they were so blinded by their pride and selfishness, they couldn't even recognize the son of God who was performing some of the most legendary miracles ever, right in front of their eyes. The bible says, pride cometh before the fall (Proverbs 16:18), and fall they did as Jesus continued to point out flaw after flaw in their behaviors and interpretation of the scriptures.

I'd venture to say that many Fanatics are probably looked at in similar light to the Pharisees. I'm not sure it's an apples to apples comparison, but there are some similarities, so I get it. Both profess to be worshippers of God, but when we look below the surface, the approach can seem more self serving than it does Christian. It may not always be pride with Fanatics, it could be lack of understanding, sensitivity or awareness, but there is still a shortcoming. I think more importantly, both had awesome opportunities to use their positions to impact unbelievers, new believers, and the whole kingdom of God, but didn't in the positive way that God would have appreciated.

Remember, the purpose of spreading God's word is not to be right, it is to save souls! Too many of us are caught up with being correct, we forget that it is easier to draw bees with honey than it is with vinegar. Who cares if you were right if you offended the person and now they really don't want to hear about God?

The silver lining is that at least fanatics still have a chance. Let's be real, there are plenty of people who weren't Pharisees and aren't Fanatics that also could have done a much better job with spreading the word or living their purpose, the difference is that Pharisees and Fanatics raise the expectation bar for themselves and everyone else around, because of an overbearing religious attitude. We have to be careful in being so heavenly focused, we are no earthly good.

#HereToServe

Numbers 5:6 - "Say to the Israelites: 'Any man or woman who wrongs another in any way and so is unfaithful to the LORD is guilty."

Just like the chapters of this book indicate, everyone is at different levels in their walk with God. From those that don't believe in Him at all, to those who are brand new in the faith or have just returned, to those who are living in complete purpose and servitude. But no matter where a person is at, we all have one thing in common, the devil is doing his best to discourage us from reaching our full potential, so we all need love and support as much as rules and judgment. Rules are important, they help to keep the order and direction God desperately wants for us. But, we also know that none of us will ever be able to follow every rule of the bible 100%, otherwise we wouldn't have needed Christ, right? That's where the loving action we mentioned earlier comes into play.

I think love may be the most underrated aspect of our Christian walk. Think about it, our society is based on some of the laws that come from the 10 commandments. Which is great, because we definitely wouldn't want people running around stealing and killing, but where is the focus on love? In the news we constantly see people debating over women's rights and people's sexual orientation. Religions oppose other religions.

Political parties are constantly at each other's throats. Some people still hate others because of skin color. <u>All these topics that many Christians argue and fight over, and yet the top 2 commandments Jesus gave had to do with love.</u> 1) Love your God with all your heart, soul and mind. 2) Love your neighbor as yourself. Now since we all have different ideas or experiences of what love is, let's see what the bible has to say about it to set the record straight.

I think the best scripture to start with regarding love is 1 John 4:8 (NIV), "Whoever does not love does not know God, because God is love." Despite being only 12 words long, this may be one of the most telling scriptures in the bible. **Not only does it confirm that we need to love, but that the very essence of God is love!** Some Fanatics hold the belief, I'm serious business. People just don't like me because I talk about God all the time. I don't care. I'm committed. But if we aren't being loving toward others, then God isn't in us. We may think we are doing God's work, but if it isn't being done in love, then it is really our own selfish ambition (1 Corinthians 16:14). This reminds me of the scripture where Jesus rebukes the people claiming to have done mighty works in His name, and He tells them, I never knew you. You may wonder why Jesus was so callous towards them. It's not that He doesn't appreciate people working for His kingdom, it's that He knows our motives and whether love is one of them. Why does love have to be the main motive, the second piece of the scripture addresses that, because God is love.

It's interesting that the scripture says, "God is love." It doesn't say that He created love, or appreciates love, it says "He is love." And doesn't that make perfect sense when you think about it. Just like we can't physically see God, we can't physically see love either. Sure we can see actions or displays of love, but you can't actually see love itself, it's just something you feel on the inside. Almost exactly like God. We may see of hear things that remind us of God, but we can't physically see Him.

It's just feeling and faith that confirms His presence in our lives. So when we say God is within us, if there is no love, then we are mistaken.

It's not by coincidence that love is the strongest emotion that keeps us on cloud nine. That's God at work. But love isn't meant to be contained for our own personal happiness, although it is important that we love ourselves. Love is meant to be given and shared. It's meant to help us connect. That's exactly what Christ was specifying with the 2 greatest commandments. Loving God with all our heart, mind and soul means connecting with Him on a much higher spiritual level so we can learn His definition of love, then give back to ourselves *and* others.

Most of our humanly experiences with love are conditional. Meaning, it changes with the conditions. God's love for us is unconditional! Meaning, it never changes! #NoMatterWhat

What is this unconditional love that God has for us? 1 Corinthians 13:4-8 gives us a perfect definition: "Love is patient, love is kind. It does not envy, it does not boast, it is not proud. It is not rude, it is not self-seeking, it is not easily angered, it keeps no record of wrongs. Love does not delight in evil but rejoices with the truth. It always protects, always trusts, always hopes, always perseveres. Love never fails." I don't know about you, but I can think of plenty of times where people have said they loved me, but their actions did not contain all of those pieces. They may have had many, or even a majority, but I guess since none of us are God, we will never have perfect love like him. BUT that shouldn't stop us from trying.

Take a second and make a list of all those traits, then do an honest evaluation of yourself to see which areas are your strengths, and which may need a little more attention and prayer.

<u>Our ability to understand and emulate God's love will have a tremendous influence on our ability to serve Him, which should always be the goal of Christianity.</u> Learning our purpose so we can serve, not so we can win arguments or prove ourselves to be holy. The more unconditional love we can give, the more people will respond to Christ, because they will be able to see Him in us, through love.

One of the most popular scriptures in the world that puts all these elements together for a perfect display of love is John 3:16. Say it with me (without reading the words) if you know it. "For God so loved the world, that he gave his only begotten son. That he would believeth in him, shall not perish but have everlasting life." When I read about Jesus' 3 years of ministry, I often get mesmerized and think how much God must love Jesus for doing all He did and never giving in to all the drama. What I should also be thinking is how much God loves me, that he sent Jesus to give me life more abundantly! Because God is love, He is showing us that love works best, when it involves giving and sacrificing for others, because God will always give it back to us. Since He is the ultimate, He made the ultimate sacrifice by giving His only son. But sacrificing doesn't necessarily mean dying like Christ did. Sacrifice could mean putting aside your opinion to let others have a turn to speak. Sacrifice may mean biting your tongue to avoid an argument or coming across as judgmental. And sacrifice could also mean putting our ego and pride to the side, and being a more humble soldier for God.

Within God's definition of love, humility stands out as one of the key traits. Look at the first eight qualities of love again: patient, kind, does not envy, does not boast, is not rude, is not self seeking, not easily angered, no record of wrongs. Of those eight mentioned, I would easily associate at least six of them with humility.

Patient. One key to humility is understanding that God created us all with our own unique characteristics and purposes. Which means we are all His children and though we are all special, not one of us is more special than the other. We all have a role to play no matter how big or small. Think of the scripture, the arm can't say it's more important the nose, etc. When we understand that everybody is different, operating at their own pace on their own path that God put them on, we should want to be patient with those who aren't at our level, and also patient with ourselves! After all, wasn't God and those who were more advanced in the word when we were still learning, patient with us?

Kind. Just being nice. Some people are so full of themselves, they never consider how they make others feel. Just being nice can help demonstrate you are compassionate toward others.

Does not envy. This definitely has to do with humility, as envy is usually a direct result of a sense of entitlement. The feeling that we deserve something someone else has. *Why do they have it and not me?* The reality is we don't know other people's hearts, their relationship and commitment to God, the history of why He may have blessed them the way He has, or if it was really God who blessed them at all! Remember, the bible asks, what profit is there for a man to gain the whole world but lose his soul (Mark 8:36)? Sometimes the material things we see people with may be the thing that absorbs their focus and keeps them out of heaven. So we should trust God that He will give us our blessings in due time. A humble servant is content with what God has given them, and doesn't sit around resenting what others have, whether it be material, spiritual, or physical. We don't have to be complacent and never ever want anything else, but we can be confident that if we leave it up to God, He will deliver at the right time.

Does not boast. Humility is all about letting go of ego. Boasting? Not so much. In fact, it's literally the exact opposite. Boasting is synonymous with bragging, or speaking with excessive pride. Boasting suggests, I did this or I know that. It makes it completely about the person speaking as if God had absolutely no influence. Boasting takes away concern/respect for all others involved in the conversation, making the speaker the central focus, which should never be our goal when trying to share the word of God with others. There is nothing wrong with being happy about everything God has done or given to you, and wanting to share with others. It just needs to be done in a tactful manner.

Is not rude. This may be one of the most common perceptions others have of Christian Fanatics. Argue too much. Don't listen. Know it all. Judgmental. All of these things add up to a verdict of rude. Rude suggests that you don't care how you address or act toward others, which clearly doesn't reflect humility. If you were to create a list of adjectives to describe Jesus, I don't think rude would be one of them. Since our actions are supposed to be modeled after Him, rude should not be associated with us either. Sure, there were times when Christ may have been a little abrupt with the Pharisees, but nowhere near what He could have been considering, you know, they were trying to kill him!

Is not self seeking. One of the most admirable qualities about humility is the ability to put others first. Being more concerned about others than we are about ourselves. Remember, Christianity is not about us, it is about serving God to bring him Glory. In fact, there are several scriptures that speak against self seeking behavior. 1) Seek ye first the kingdom of God (Matthew 6:33). 2) Take no worry as to what you will eat (Matthew 6:25). 3) How much more will your Father in heaven give you good things (Luke 11:13). The bible makes it very clear that we can focus on helping others, because God will take care of us. So it's only a lack of humility that leads us to act contrary to God's instruction.

Not easily angered. This is similar to patient. Not only does the book of proverbs speak about not losing your temper (Proverbs 29:11), humility tells us that we really have no right to get easily angered with others, because God never gets easily angered with us despite our flaws and mistakes.

Keeps no record of wrongs. Forgiveness is written everywhere, including the Lord's prayer: "Forgive us our debts as we have forgiven our debtors." Humility means accepting people as they are, and that even means the mistakes they will make against you. Let's be clear, humility doesn't mean being foolish. Sometimes you have to walk away or distance yourself from people, but that's a different story. Really, keeping no record of wrongs is just as beneficial to our own personal peace of mind as it is to the person we are forgiving.

At the end of the day, humility means less of us, and more of God. #Decrease2Increase

If we aren't pushing ourselves to serve Him by following His commands, then have we really humbled ourselves as much as we need to? We mentioned earlier that one of the best qualities of a Fanatic is the recognition that God is all supreme, so it's important not to contradict that with actions or words that don't reflect our humility for how much He does/did/going to do for us, and how much we will use that to do for others as a servant.

We all need love. If any of us were to fall off a bike and seriously hurt ourselves, I'm sure we would want someone to console and help us feel better, not give us a lecture on balance and pedaling. And that is exactly the difference between demonstrating Christian love versus enforcing Christian law. **Yes, law is needed, but without love, trust me, nobody will listen anyway.**

That is why the bible says spirit and in truth (John 4:24). The law is the truth, but if it doesn't come from a genuine and compassionate spirit, then it really isn't what God called for. God wants everyone exposed to His word, but He also wants their freedom of choice to be honored.

As a representative of God, we must strive to represent Him in all aspects, including people's right to choose. How many scriptures in the New Testament have you read about Jesus arguing with people? Aside from the Pharisees, who usually instigated some type of confrontation, there aren't many accounts of Jesus getting upset or yelling when talking about God to others. Why? Because a truly knowledgeable person isn't afraid to have conversations about Christianity with those of other beliefs, because we are secure in our deep roots and know we will not be swayed easily. And if we want others to develop roots, we first have to plant the seed. If you know anything about farming, which I don't, but I do know you can't plant a seed in hard ground. It has to be softened up first. Kindness is much more likely to soften up a heart to plant a seed in then harsh words. That's why we simply present what we know, and let God do the rest. **So if you find yourself getting annoyed or argumentative, looking around church to see who's coming and who's wearing what, always talking about helping others with their problems but dodging your own, never being able to answer a question or hold a conversation without forcing God into the mix, you may want to seek God's counsel if you are really ready to minister to others.** The word says don't grieve the Holy Spirit (Ephesians 4:30) and we definitely don't want to grieve others. You didn't see Jesus going around yelling and arguing at people, so neither should we. Let's not be guilty of spreading Page Rage in conversations that could've helped others realize the love of Christ.

Being a Christian is all about God's grace. We don't want to set unrealistic expectations of perfection that will turn people away. Don't be a gavel banger. You may have people on the verge of converting to Christianity or others who stepped away from the faith (for whatever reason) and are now returning. Let's embrace them all the way Christ would and not make them feel intimidated as if they aren't ready to walk with Christ, because they are too scared of messing up. **We want them to understand that messing up doesn't mean God cuts you off, it means His grace covers the mistake**. But if we in the church display an attitude of condemnation, they won't ever feel the love of God that is supposed to flow through us to them. Let's skip the, "Go to Hell. Go directly to Hell and do not pass go," speeches. Let's not make others feel defensive or neglected because we are too consumed with our own personal agenda. The devil already causes enough scorn and stress, and God's promises definitely should not be a source of stress for anyone. His promises call for rejoicing and praise! Our faith may not be where it needs to be if we are causing more angst than joy for God! Remember, God called us all to be stewards of His word, and nothing shows that more than our actions. So let's thank God for opening our spirit and minds to His greatness, while remembering to open our hearts to others.

NOTES:

CONCLUSION

Despite the subtitle, Christianity is no simple subject. We just covered some of the basics to make sure the foundation was solid, but really there is so much more to learn if we truly want to understand Christ. Once we decide to serve Him, the process really never stops! But maybe you're Not a Christian, maybe Your Parents are but you aren't sure, or maybe you're just exploring it. I hope these pages gave you a little insight from a non-confrontational view and encouraged you to seek out more information. Don't be afraid to search for positive experiences and conversations about Christianity. There are plenty of Christians out there who appreciate open dialogue as much as anyone else. Let's be honest, there are people of all walks that don't know how to engage in healthy banter, it's not isolated to just Christians. Look for the good, ignore the bad, and just know that Jesus loves us all.

If you're saved, comfortable or a fanatic, I pray that Christ continues to work in your life to take you even higher. We are living in very different times, and many Christian scholars even believe we are in the last days that the bible prophesizes. Christianity needs servants more than ever to be representatives the way God intended. Just remember, if we aren't embedding love in our service, it's all for nothing .

So, what type of Christian am I, you may ask, especially after doing all of this talking. Well, if nothing else I'm the type that would take years of learning, education, prayer, fellowship, fasting, bible study, praise, travelling, crying, anger, listening, trying, failing, trying some more and sacrificing the time necessary to type it up for others, and realize this is something I need to do in service to the God who created the universe and who has never let me get too lost in it.

If never before and never again, this time I got it right. And you have too! Because no matter what kind of Christian level you related to the most, you related, and there is always room for you to grow from there!

Be encouraged. Be blessed!

FINAL NOTES:

5 STAPLES of SPIRITUALITY:
Bible study
Prayer
Praise and worship
Fellowship
Fasting

VOCABULARY

Pray.D.H.D – when you convince yourself to pray, and within minutes your thoughts are more distracted and random than scrolling through a Twitter news feed. 5 minutes later you realize you were in the middle of a prayer and didn't even finish!

Gavel banging – Those that are still upholding the law even though court was closed centuries ago when Jesus died

BiQuil– When you try to read the bible at night and it puts you right to sleep. But, better to fall asleep with the word than something crazy!

Squinting - judging Christianity by what some people say or do, rather than what the bible explains. generalizing all Christians into the same group based on limited personal experience

Hide n go Creep - When you're doing things you know you shouldn't be doing, so you stay away from praying and God as if he can't see you

Page Rage – stressing one page or scripture from the bible, rather than keeping everything in context

Spiritual Bulimia – praying and then worrying, which completely pushes out your faith

Servant's breath - breathe in and imagine the entire universe. All the planets and living creations that have ever existed. Feel God's presence in and all around, not just in heaven. Recognize the life and power being given to complete your tasks. Inhale greatness. Exhale miracles. There is no gravity, just complete release in God's Spirit.

Miracle Faith – not minimizing what God can do. Expecting miracles despite all the doubt from others around you. Not being afraid to speak on and work towards the unexplainable things God can do.

For other faith filled reading, be sure to check out:

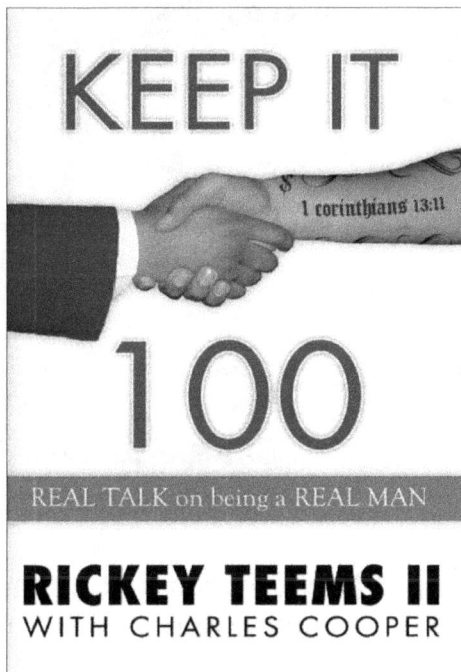

KEEP IT
1 corinthians 13:11
100
REAL TALK on being a REAL MAN

RICKEY TEEMS II
WITH CHARLES COOPER

Every young man needs to learn how to become a grown man. Every grown man should strive to become a better man. Wouldn't it be great if there was a practical source to provide us with insightful and entertaining information on the critical concepts of manhood? Well, Keeping it 100: Real Talk on being a Real Man, is that fresh and motivating look at what it takes for every man to reach his pinnacle. Good is good, but learning to function at 100% of your purpose and potential is the only way to obtain GREAT. 100% of the success you envision! 100% of the blessings you deserve! 100% of the dreams and life most people only wish for! From finances and females to God and goals, Keeping it 100 covers the essential spiritual, financial, psychological, emotional, and social bottom lines that every young man should know to establish the strongest foundation possible for adulthood. This isn't your grandfather's book! It is current, it is innovative, and it is you!

Harry and Sherry discover that just because we can't see God, doesn't mean He isn't there!

- "The authors do an amazing job explaining God to the reader."

- "Every Sunday school teacher, church, parent who wants to introduce a child or adult to God must have this book."

- "Not only fun to read but educational too."

www.noguilebooks.com

About the Author:

Rickey Teems II is a US Air Force veteran who graduated with honors in both Psychology (Bachelors Degree) and Marriage & Family Therapy (Masters Degree). Teems is an active counselor who specializes in family and young adult practice. Teems also volunteers in various mentor groups and church ministry, and is a highly sought after public speaker due to his wonderful combination of humor, insight and compassion. Teems has authored additional family and young adult books such as, "Keep it 100," "Unshakeable Faith," and, "Why Can't We See God?" For more information or to book a visit from Teems, be sure to visit:

www.noguilebooks.com

www.ingramcontent.com/pod-product-compliance
Lightning Source LLC
Chambersburg PA
CBHW071553040426
42452CB00008B/1152